Compact Disc-Interactive:
A Designer's Overview

COMPACT DISC-INTERACTIVE

A Designer's Overview

Edited by Philips International

McGRAW-HILL BOOK COMPANY

New York   St. Louis   San Francisco   Auckland   Montreal
New Delhi   Singapore   Sydney   Tokyo   Toronto

Library of Congress Cataloging-in-Publication Data

Compact disc-interactive.

Includes index.
1. CD-I technology. I. Philips International.
TK7882.C56C65 1988   621.397'6   88-2735
ISBN 0-07-049816-4

This book is a simultaneous
co-publication with Kluwer Technische
Boeken, Deventer, The Netherlands.
Printed and bound in the U.S. by R.R. Donnelley & Sons Company.

ISBN 0-07-049816-4

1234567890   DOC/DOC   8921098

FOREWORD BY D.C. GEEST

I am very pleased to be able to present this book, 'CD-I: A Designer's Overview' to you. We in Philips see CD-I as one of the most exciting challenges yet. CD-I builds on the success of Compact Disc-Digital Audio, and further extends the use of the compact disc. It combines high quality video images and full color animation with various quality levels of sound, as well as text and database software - a truly multi-media system. CD-I is based on a worldwide specification, in the same way as CD-Digital Audio. Indeed, CD-I players can also play CD-Audio discs, ensuring complete compatibility with the existing repertoire of audio CD's.

But the establishment of a specification, and the building of CD-I players is only one part of the picture. The other essential element is the software - the range of CD-I discs that will join the players to form the basis of a new publishing industry. It is the purpose of this book to help those interested in participating in this new industry to understand the possibilities and techniques of CD-I, as well as to appreciate the basics of CD-I disc design.

This book is a summary of knowledge on CD-I, taken from the many sources within the Philips company, as well as from our associated companies throughout the world. Apart from those within Philips and Sony, as well as in Matsushita, who were responsible for the actual CD-I Specification, I would like also specifically to acknowledge the assistance of American Interactive Media in Los Angeles, New Media Projects in London, and members of my own staff here in Eindhoven. The individuals who contributed to the actual writing of the book are too numerous to mention individually, but without their efforts, this book would not have come about.

D.C.Geest
Senior Managing Director
and Chairman
Corporate Group - Home Interactive Systems
Philips International B.V.

PREFACE TO SECOND EDITION

This book is an introduction to CD-I. It has been written to provide an overview of the current state of development for those who want to know more about the topic - perhaps with an ambition to become CD-I publishers or to become CD-I designers.

It is not a designer's guide. That is, it cannot be used as a vademecum while designing a CD-I disc. At the time of writing there is an insufficient body of experience to enable such a guide to be written - only two CD-I discs have been displayed to Licensees, one by Sony in June 1987 and one by Philips in December 1987. The book does, however, represent the cumulative experience of most of those already involved in CD-I.

It is likely that the book will go through many revisions as the body of experience grows and many of our expectations are either confirmed or denied. The long term success of CD-I is going to be determined by the foresight of the publisher and the ingenuity of the designer; so the more experience can be shared at this stage, the greater the effort that can go into original design work. The reader is therefore invited to write to the editor (c/o the publisher) with comments and criticisms so that subsequent editions may be both more informative and more comprehensive.

This second edition has been edited by Dick Fletcher of New Media Projects in London. The substantial revisions to the first edition have been made possible in particular by the guidance and detailed comments of:

Richard Bruno of Optimage in Chicago
Peter Cook of Grolier Electronic Publishing in New York
Peter Essink of Japan New Media Systems in Tokyo
Nicholas Lewis of New Media Projects in London
Graham Sharpless of Home Interactive Systems in Eindhoven

J.M. Preston
Philips International
Eindhoven

1 March 1988

TABLE OF CONTENTS

HOW TO USE THIS BOOK

This guide has been designed to accommodate a variety of readers' needs and interests. It is anticipated that some people will need to study in depth, while others will want only an introduction. Even those who will eventually study the entire guide may read selectively at first, to gain a solid background before coming to grips with the finer details.

The book grows more technical as it progresses. The seven chapters break down this way:

Chapter 1 explains the concepts of multi-media and interactivity.

Chapter 2 offers a general background to electronic publishing and optical disc technology. The CD-I player and disc are described, together with the principal audio-visual features of the system.

Chapter 3 looks at the audio-visual side of the technology in more detail, and explains what CD-I can do, and the design implications of its many features.

Chapter 4 looks critically at the kind of questions the potential designer must ask before undertaking a CD-I project and designing the brief.

Chapter 5 discusses the design process in some detail, and describes essential stages and production tasks.

Chapter 6 presents a range of hypothetical projects which might be among the first CD-I discs on the market: a multi-media encyclopedia, a pop music program, a language program, and several different game styles. Some of the various features and design considerations unique to CD-I are illustrated by specific examples within each application.

Chapter 7 discusses the technology in depth, from a computing perspective, and describes elements of the player and the technical composition of the disc itself.

While the book flows logically from Chapter 1 to Chapter 7, readers with different needs and interests may want to approach the guide itself 'interactively'.

Chapters 1 and 2 provide a general introduction and are appropriate for senior management and strategists.

It is likely that the potential CD-I designer or producer will read the whole book, but may wish to begin with the first two chapters for a conceptual introduction, and skip to Chapter 6 to look at how typical applications might work. Many may then prefer to think about the design process described in Chapters 4 and 5 before tackling the technical material.

What to look for
- Chapter 1: multimedia and interactivity
- Chapter 2: optical publishing panorama
- Chapter 3: the media palette
- Chapter 4: some pre-design questions
- Chapter 5: design considerations
- Chapter 6: some CD-I examples
- Chapter 7: inside the technical system
- Appendices:
    - Glossary
    - CD-RTOS and InVision
    - Index

Because this guide covers so much inter-related material - such as the description of a feature from both a design and a technical point of view - it contains aids to help readers cross-reference new ideas and concepts as they appear in different contexts. These include:

- Side comments to help identify cross references.
- A Glossary explaining key words and concepts at the end of the book.
- An Index covering all references to important words and phrases.

CHAPTER 1: INTRODUCTION

This chapter introduces the two basic concepts behind Compact Disc-Interactive (CD-I), the most recent development in the tradition of optical disc recording - multi-media and interactivity.

CD-I: TRUE MULTI-MEDIA TECHNOLOGY

Compact Disc-Interactive (CD-I) will be the first publishing medium to bring the world of multi-media to a broad general audience. It is essential for the CD-I publisher, designer and producer to understand this concept, and why CD-I is so much better suited to multi-media applications than other technology.

WHAT IS MULTI-MEDIA?

The term multi-media originated with the audio-visual industry, to describe a computer-controlled, multiple-projector slide show with a sound track. In computer terms, multi-media is viewed as a blending of media types: text, audio, visual, and computer data in one convenient delivery medium. Although CD-I is not the only combination of hardware and software capable of delivering multi-media information, it is the first to do so in a highly standardized form - and, for broad acceptance of a technological concept such as multi-media, system standards are a prerequisite. CD-I has been defined as a system standard, in contrast to CD-ROM which functions simply as a peripheral to a system. The CD-I specification defines how the information is stored on the CD-I optical disc, exemplifies how it is encoded in the recording studios, and defines how it is decoded in the player. A peripheral such as CD-ROM defines only how the information is stored on the disc, making international agreement on recorder and player standards impossible.

Why is Multi-media Important?

Information sources such as books, periodicals, film, television, radio, video, LPs, cassettes, and computer software, have evolved along various tracks and, in our minds, are viewed as separate and distinct media. But information need not be defined by the medium in which it is presented. The development of CD-I enable us for the first time to mix information from a variety of sources, using the medium most appropriate to the message - a short sequence of images called a video clip, computer animation, or a screen full of text, all supported by any combination of speech, music and sound effect as needed. CD-I combines the best creative concepts from book design, film and video production, sound recording, and software design. This represents a new range of challenges for the designer, who must select the most effective combinations from the rich media palette of CD-I.

Multi-media CD-ROM

CD-I is an optical disc technology, the logical extension of both the Compact Disc and Interactive LaserVision. In 1985, CD-ROM (Compact Disc-Read Only Memory) was introduced as a mass storage peripheral for personal computers (PCs). Though developed primarily for text, it can store digital data of any kind, including sound and graphics. However, the multi-media potential of CD-ROM is defined by processing power, audio output, and the display capabilities of the computer that is controlling the CD-ROM drive. While most PCs can generate adequate audio and graphics output for computer applications, they were not designed to produce high quality audio or to display natural video images. CD-ROM is nevertheless well suited to dedicated solutions, where internationally agreed standards do not play a significant role.

The limitations of the computer can be overcome (newer machines such as the Amiga, IBM PS2 and Macintosh II, go some way towards addressing these shortcomings), but a lack of standards is likely to create many different hardware and software methods for implementing multi-media CD-ROM. As a result, the technology is likely to be confined to 'niche' markets such as spare parts catalogs, text databases, and specialist graphics applications.

Digital Video Interactive (DVI)

Digital Video Interactive (DVI) is one widely publicized approach to the decoding of audio-visual materials. It is a custom chip technology that allows, amongst other features, the compression of one hour of VHS quality partial screen full motion video on a single CD-ROM disc. It is anticipated that DVI technology will initially be marketed as a chip set on a series of dedicated graphics and audio boards for AT class computers. So, unlike CD-I, it is not a stand alone solution. It has no international system agreement, and is not intended yet to be in a price bracket appropriate to consumer applications.

LaserVision

With the commercial introduction of LaserVision in the 1970s, many pioneers in the computer industry saw the opportunity to combine the audio-visual riches of videodisc with the processing power of the personal computer. The result was interactive video (IV), a multi-media hybrid that uses the videodisc as a computer peripheral.

In interactive video, computer software stored on a floppy or hard disc generates text and graphics, and controls the access of sound and images from the videodisc - in response to actions of the person in front of the screen (who may be using a keyboard, mouse, touch-screen or other device). Interactive LaserVision has developed as a specialist's technology, particularly effective for training and point-of-sales materials. Despite this success, it has not penetrated into the broader markets of education and the home to any significant degree, because of the high cost of the hardware, and a lack of standards for both hardware and software.

CD-I and Multi-media

Unlike the videodisc and CD-ROM, CD-I has been designed for multi-media consumer applications. Its technological premise is the complete integration of all media types. How CD-I achieves this, and the full range of CD-I multi-media capabilities are fully explained in the chapters that follow.

BEYOND MULTI-MEDIA: HYPER-MEDIA

The concept of hyper-media could have been invented to describe CD-I. Its origins lie in the notion of hyper-text, a term coined by computer guru Ted Nelson in 1965 as a method of linking related bodies of information to allow the user to browse through different databases randomly. Owl International's 'Guide' and Apple Computer's 'HyperCard' are two recent software products that embody these notions. Creative software designers are now using these same concepts to link different kinds of media - hence the term hyper-media.

How does hyper-media work? An example can be taken from the Grolier Multi-media Encyclopedia project, which uses a hyper-media approach to integrate separate text, audio and visual databases. In this product, the user can access the text of an article - say, the biography of Abraham Lincoln - and use simple features of the system to find pictures of Lincoln, orreadings of Lincoln's famous speeches.

This article in turn may be linked to a 'Time Machine' database of historical events, which might lead the curious users to, say, the history of portraiture or photography and from there to a fully narrated audio-visual essay, and so on.

All this must of course be defined by the design team - clearly, a massive task when an encyclopedia is involved - but the concept is a relatively simple one. With CD-I, you can link any type of audio, video and text information on the disc to any other.

INTERACTIVITY - THE 'I' IN CD-I

CD-I is founded on the concept of interactivity - that is, providing the user with a means to interact with a program in a meaningful and rewarding way. The success of the CD-I designer in developing compelling interactive programs will ultimately dictate the success of CD-I in the marketplace.

What is Interactivity ?

There are probably as many answers to this question as there are interactive applications. Using an automatic bank-teller machine, playing an arcade game, entering figures into a spreadsheet program, accessing information in an on-line database - all these are examples of interaction with a fully computer-controlled device. In CD-I terms, interactivity is the method used to interact with the content of a program which has been designed to respond in a very specific way to each decision, choice or request made by the user.

The CD-I designer's role is to balance the objectives of the application with the degree of interactive control that is to be provided to the user. This balance must be carefullly struck at all times - while a flight simulator game might require continuous interaction from the user, an instructional program or pop music disc might only require occasional stopping and starting. (Remember, the user will purchase a CD-I disc for its content, not to get a sore thumb pressing buttons!)

How to use Interactivity

There is no magic formula for developing good interactive programs, although a full understanding of both the program's content and the user's needs and desires is a prerequisite. The interactive video experience can suggest some rules for the levels of challenge, reward, review and so forth which can be useful for certain kinds of program.

However, in general, only one rule need apply: whatever the goal of the program, make the journey to get there - the pathway through the content - as interesting and compelling as possible. The TV screen directed by a remote control device (a mouse, keypad or joystick) is the door into the content. It is the designer's task to help the user step through that door and become immersed in a unique experience.

Interactivity: The Educator

Virtually all the experience for developing interactive materials (besides video games) comes from the development of educational computer software and interactive video. Educators have long known that interaction with audio-visual learning materials enhances the information transfer.

The success of interactive LaserVision training materials compared to traditional training methods is still further evidence of the potential for well-developed interactive programs.

Reports from training professionals indicate as much as a 40%increase in retention can be gained over standard training techniques. In an interactive program, the user is in firm control of the level and pace of instruction, and actively engaged in the pursuit of knowledge.

However, the motivation of the student and the job trainee are quite different from that of the average consumer, who is looking for entertainment or information, but is not compelled to enjoy and benefit from the experience. Consumers will not buy CD-I discs to get good grades (although a CD-I SAT disc could prove the exception!).

Do Consumers want Interactive Programs?

Some observers have remarked that consumers do not want to interact with their TV sets. Are they right? We do not yet know. Although a clear case for interactivity can be made in the training and education markets, nothing quite like CD-I has ever been offered consumers before, and no body of research exists to supply us with an answer. The best market feedback on which to base conjecture is the experience with video games and home computers. For a short period video games were phenominally successful but, limited to 'shoot 'em up' games with primitive graphics, they proved a passing fad. The early home computers also failed to live up to consumers' expectations and quickly joined the video games at the back of the closet.

Were these marketing disasters a fair test of the viability of interactivity in the home? Hardly: it was too much to expect simple video games to have any lasting value, and the software produced for the early home computers was limited by the inadequate processing power and data storage capabilities of the hardware, and the crudity of their visual displays.

CD-I does not have these limitations. With its inherent multi-media capabilities, massive storage capacity, and the powerful processors built into the player, CD-I provides a system for software performance which is well beyond existing home computer systems. With high quality sound and video pictures, CD-I represents a new information resource, delivering interactive programs on a wide range of topics and subject areas. CD-I should appeal to the same variety of interests that drive the sales of millions of books and magazines - certainly no previous generation of software has had this capability.

There are categories of CD-I software that we cannot yet begin to imagine, new combinations of information and entertainment waiting to be invented. The fertile minds of the creative community will respond to the challenge and opportunities of CD-I - the most powerful information system ever known.

CHAPTER 2: THE BACKGROUND OF CD-I

The last chapter introduced the key concepts behind CD-I technology - interactivity and multi-media. This chapter presents an overview of optical disc technology, and CD-I (Compact Disc-Interactive) in particular. It traces the history of the medium and explains the different kinds of Compact Disc (CD) now available - CD-DA, CD-ROM, CD-V and CD-I. It also describes, in general terms, the technical and creative aspects of CD-I discussed in later chapters, as well as the market opportunities for this exciting new medium.

This chapter is essential reading both for those who intend to study this guide thoroughly - designers, programmers and others preparing to make CD-I software - and those who need only a conceptual overview - presidents and vice presidents, administrators, marketing executives and others not directly involved in the job of production.

THOSE CHILLY SATURDAYS

First, an imaginary look at CD-I as we may soon know it. Picture a Saturday afternoon in the late autumn. Wintery clouds block the pale sun, the air is crisp and cold. The chores are done for the day, (except to rake, once again, the eternally falling leaves) and there's nothing left to do for a couple of hours. It's a perfect time for sport. But, the summer sports have finished, there's nothing on TV until tonight, and outside - nothing but fond recollections of warm days on the golf course.

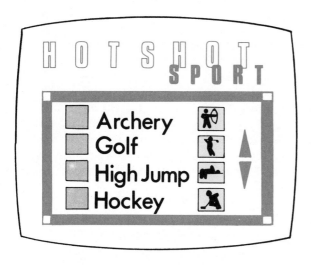

What a perfect time to try out that new edition of the CD-I golf game you picked up at the supermarket this morning. A few preparations are in order first - a snack, a soft drink, your favourite chair. Then, slap the compact disc in the player, and you're off to the sunshine again.

So where to go? Slide through a few of those good-looking choice frames ... Hot Shot Sport! Yes, that's you - look out Jack Nicklaus, here you come. You select golf from the list. Now choose a course. There are several on the disc, but the main thing today is to find sun and heat, so why not go for the big one ... that's it ... the Augusta National, home of the Masters. It's a chance to challenge golf's greats - and it's always warm in Georgia.

Chapter 6: Hot Shot Sports for Design Considerations

Before you tackle eighteen holes, why not sit back, finish off that hotdog while watching a 'mini-movie' about one of the most famous courses in the world. That'll get you in the mood, and besides you wouldn't want to smear mustard on the putter!

Because the CD-I system is both a computer and a television, you have the best of both. The huge storage capacity of the disc offers a total experience in action and pictures. On the one hand, you can play golf with the interactive computer game: choose a whole round or a few holes. Whatever control device you use - keypad, mouse or any other - you have complete control over the animated figure on the screen, position, swing speed and precise moment of impact between the club and the ball.

On the other hand, with CD-I, the computer-animated character is combined with real photographic views of the fairway. The background is not a crude computer-generated graphic, but a series of actual shots of a world-famous course. CD-I also offers realistic high quality sound, to heighten the sensation: if you want to imagine yourself in a tournament, CD-I will even provide spectators who will follow your game with interest and appreciation!

You don't have to work at it. If you need a break from the stress of serious tournament golf, you can relax with some narrated video sequences about the course. They describe the history, course layout, and some of the great golf moments that have happened there. What a thrill to play a round on one of the most famous courses in the world - from your armchair, CD-I style.

The technology that can take a golf lover to Augusta or St. Andrews could equally take an amateur archaeologist through the Pyramids or an Etruscan tomb - or a gourmet cook into the great restaurants of the world for lessons from their master chefs - or a pop music fan into the studio to create whole new videos to their favourite tracks.

All this is possible through a machine no larger or more demanding than your VCR. CD-I truly combines entertainment with education, information with recreation, in a form that the whole family can use and enjoy for years to come. CD-I may seem like the technology of the future, but all this is possible now - because of work that began over twenty years ago.

ELECTRONIC PUBLISHING

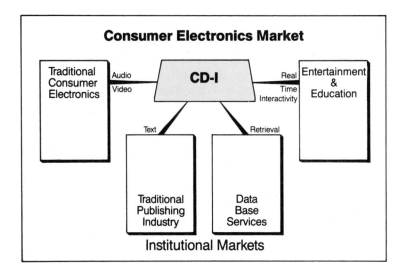

The concept of publishing - that is, the distribution of information in printed form - has altered little over the centuries, even if production processes have changed greatly. However, the evolution of new communication media - radio, film, television, audio and video recording, as well as computing and telecommunications - has effected changes which now present wholly new concepts.

The one feature these new media have in common is that they are stored and delivered in forms that can only be read by a machine. They are unintelligible to the naked eye. The concept has grown from punched paper tapes and cards to magnetic tapes and discs, from factory automation to telecommunications and mass data storage, from entertainment through to every facet of information management. It is now possible to exchange information instantaneously, worldwide.

Yet only recently has electronic publishing touched the world of print, with the introduction of computer softwareand live on-line databases. These have tended to be used for large volumes of information - typically, financial, scientific or legal. It remained for optical digital discs to introduce the concept to popular communications.

OPTICAL DISCS

Optical disc technology represents a great leap forward in the quality, quantity and variety of data that can be stored,and what can be done with that recorded information. Furthermore, optical discs are robust, virtually impossible to pirate and so versatile that the technology has spawned an enormous variety of consumer and specialist applications.

The original research program led to three product development projects. The first of these involved data collection for company archival systems. This resulted in the Megadoc system which was the forerunner of the current Write Once Read Many (WORM) drives.

The other two development paths (leading to Compact Disc and LaserVision) were for distribution systems. So disc encoding and replication processes had to be developed as well.

The larger storage capacities and lower cost of production of optical discs resulted in the Compact Disc - Audio (CD-DA) breakthrough. However, optical media have been on the market since 1978 with LaserVision. This video version of optical storage has found success in the educational world in the form of interactive video discs. The digital compact audio disc (CD-DA) was launched in 1982 and has proved highly successful in the music listening world.

Optical media devices can be divided into two categories:

- Peripheral Devices: devices that can read the optical disc and transfer the contents read to an external decoder.

- Systems: devices that both read and decode the contents of the optical disc.

Both LaserVision and CD-DA from inception were conceived as systems.

Each of these types of device were originally intended for passive use. The 'systems' family was extended in March 1987 with CD-I and in July 1987 with CD-Video (CD-V is an amalgam of LaserVision and CD-DA technologies, with a digital audio track added to the LaserVision disc).

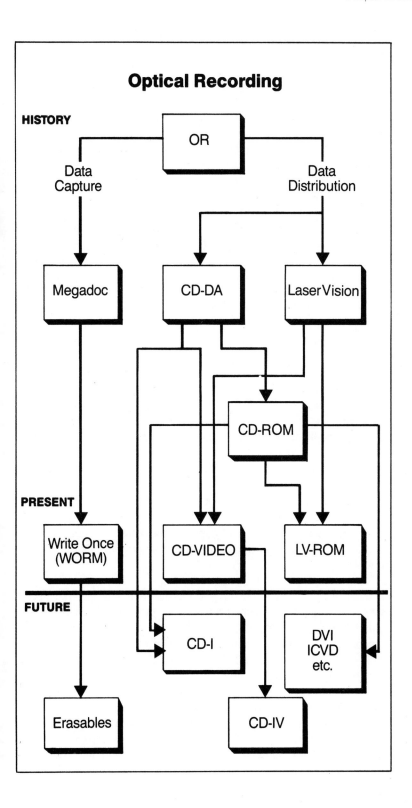

The original LaserVision and CD-DA specifications were also extended to form the 'peripheral' family branch with the introduction of CD-ROM in June 1985 and LaserVision-ROM shortly afterwards.

Both peripheral and system variations are 'read only' media, though only CD-ROM and LaserVision-ROM are named as such. There is a great deal of commonality among the LaserVision derivatives and among the CD-DA derivatives such as the same basic disc mastering and replication processes, and commonality of players for tracking and reading disc-bound information.

The use of optical media, like that of many other types of product, ranges from passive linear applications to fully interactive applications.

Existing media products like film and gramophone records could be regarded as fully passive. Television with a remote control keypad has a minimum level of interactivity requiring actions as simple as changing the channel. The use of other types of product ranges from passive use to full real-time interactivity in something like an automobile.

Optical read-only products span the same range. CD-DA for music listening, and LaserVision discs for films are fully passive products. At the other extreme are the interactive products of CD-ROM text databases, the interactive videodisc programs used in education and training, and the fully interactive consumer products of CD-Interactive.

All optical discs, whether intended for passive or interactive use, are based on the same principles. Coded information from a master recording on magnetic tape is burnt into a specially-coated glass master disc by a powerful laser beam. The beam records digital signals as a pattern of shallow pits and grooves on a long spiral path - rather like a conventional audio LP, but much, much denser (and winding outwards rather than inwards).

A series of copies taken from this glass master creates the metal stampers which are used to press copies in a special plastic. A fine film of reflective aluminium is laid over this, and sealed under a tough, clear plastic topcoat: this allows the aluminium to shine through, but protects the data well away from dangers of dirt, wear or rough handling. Optical discs are virtually impervious to damage.

A low-powered laser in the reading head of the disc player bounces a fine beam of light off the reflective surface of the disc through a network of prisms and mirrors to a photodiode which decodes variations in reflected light into audio and video signals, and computer data. The output of the player itself is compatible with existing domestic audio and video equipment.

COMPACT DISC (CD)

The Compact Disc (CD) is one type of optical disc technology. It offers a choice of formats for data of different kinds: CD-Digital Audio (CD-DA) for top-quality sound recording, CD-Video (CD-V) for video clips, CD-Read Only Memory (CD-ROM) for high-volume computer data storage and retrieval, and CD-Interactive (CD-I) for the first fully interactive combination of sound and pictures, computer text and graphics on one system.

- CD-DA audio discs measure 12cm (4.75") across, andcan carry up to 72 minutes of top-quality digital audio per side.

- CD-V discs range from a 12cm 'single' with six minutes' video and 20 minutes' audio to 20cm and 30cm (8" and 12") discs offering 20 minutes and one hour of video per side respectively.

- CD-ROM discs are essentially computer storage media, holding up to 600Mb of data on a 12cm disc - 150,000 pages' worth of text information and enough, say, for the complete white and yellow pages of the whole of the East Coast of the United States.

- CD-I will hold up to 650Mb on a 12cm disc, but can handle data from a variety of source media, including natural video still frames (over 7800), audio (over 2 hours of top-quality sound or about 17 hours of simple narration), text and graphics (up to 150,000 pages' worth) or, more typically, a combination of these under the control of the computer program also stored on the disc.

COMPACT DISC-DIGITAL AUDIO (CD-DA)

Compact Disc-Digital Audio (CD-DA) - what most people now know as 'compact disc' - is the most successful consumer product of the decade. CD-DA was launched in 1982 and by the end of 1987 about 30 million players and 450 million discs will have been delivered worldwide, with current manufacturing capacity for over 100M discs a year. Consumers embraced the new product because it offered very high quality sound reproduction at an attractive price: as the next compact disc systems emerge, offering multi-media and interactivity, the effects will be as revolutionary as the emergence of sound and picture recording themselves.

All CD technical specifications are based on CD-DA to ensure maximum compatibility as the newer products come onto the market: the same plants can make discs for all formats, the new CD-V and CD-I machines will play CD-DA discs.

ANALOG AND DIGITAL

Whereas other audio-visual media employ analog recording technology, based on variations in electrical current, CD-DA, CD-ROM and CD-I compact discs use digital techniques based on the more precise binary computer code.

The striking difference between a compact audio disc and conventional LPs and tapes illustrates one advantage of digital technology: the digitally encoded compact disc is virtually free from the degradation or 'noise' inevitable in analog systems. This means not only crisper, cleaner audio recordings, but also a medium reliable enough to carry computer data as well as audio-visual signals.

INTERNATIONAL STANDARDS

To be compatible with existing television receivers and video monitors, both videotape (VCR) and LaserVision are tied to national television broadcast standards. This analog technology varies in both the transmission of the basic video signal and its color-coding. A tape or discmade for America, for example, cannot be played on a machine purchased in Europe.

Chapter 3: National Television Broadcast Standards

What distinguishes CD-I as an audio-visual medium is that, like CD-DA, it is internationally compatible at its most basic level. As a result any disc will work in any player, anywhere in the world. CD-I employs digital technology. Wherever the system may be, a decoder within the player adapts the video signal to the type of receiver or monitor to which it is linked.

Furthermore, the standard was established by two leading manufacturers, Philips and Sony, who have licensed over 150 other companies to make discs and players.

Technically, this makes a CD-I disc as universal as a book or audio recording. However, CD-I has another feature: one disc can hold enough data to present the same material in several languages. Sound, pictures, text, graphics and computer programming are stored separately, and only mixed within the player during the actual presentation.

The disc's large and flexible storage capacity can thus handle the text, pictures and sound to present a substantial program in a choice of national languages.

COMPACT DISC-INTERACTIVE (CD-I)

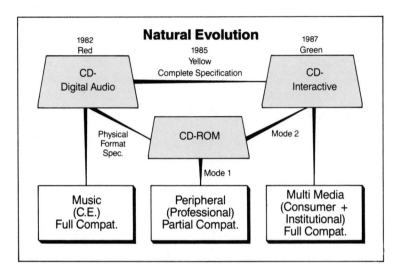

The CD-I Full Functional Specification, or Green Book, was issued in March 1987. Amongst a number of 'logical requirements', the following stand out:

- Compatibility with the CD-DA specifications (the Red Book), so that a CD-I player can handle all CD-DA discs; (some CD-ROM and some more recent CD-DA players can also be upgraded to CD-I).

- Compatibility with existing consumer electronic products so the new CD-I player can not only send sound through a home stereo, but also pictures as well as sound through the home TV.

- The entire interactive multi-media presentation must be contained on one CD-I disc for playback on a CD-I player - unlike interactive LaserVison, there need be no extra computer and software.

- 'Future proof' technology that takes account of new and proposed standards, and allows room for later enhancements.

THE CD-I PLAYER

The CD-I specification defines the minimum standard or base case. This may be an integrated CD-I system or a separate decoder (or 'black box') to upgrade an existing CD-DA player. The basic drive is identical in all compact disc players and includes control circuitry for the laser read-out head.

At the heart of the CD-I player is its operating system. This controls the rest of the system. CD-RTOS, Compact Disc - Real-Time Operating System, was developed to presentinteractive multi-media in 'real-time' - that is, in direct response to the user in front of the screen.

Appendix C: CD-RTOS

The CD-RTOS, held in the player's memory handles the basic management of the system, including the synchronization of audio, video, text, graphics and computer data pouring in from various sources for decoding and co-ordination into the final presentation on the screen.

On all compact discs, information is organized in tracks and sectors. Typically, on a CD-I disc all the material in one application is held in one track, which comprises many small sectors of individual audio, video and text. These sectors are played through the system at 75 per second. What appears on the screen, or is heard through the loud speaker, depends therefore on what these sectors contain. If they are full of audio, there will be no new pictures arriving at the screen; if they are full of video pictures, there can be no sound. So the effective CD-I producer must learn to balance the creative requirements of his program with the rate at which sectors can be played back - the amount of space available in the data channel. It is therefore essential for the producer to come to an early understanding both of the features available for program making and what space in the data channel each individual feature takes up.

CD-I AUDIO

CD-I offers a choice of quality levels for both audio and video: higher levels produce higher quality, but take up more space in the memory banks and in the data channels which send information from the disc to the player. The choice of quality level is vital since CD-I must typically handle a variety of data at any one time.

CD-I offers six audio options - three sound quality levels in either mono or stereo: A-Level (mono and stereo) is equivalent to the first play of a brand new high quality audio LP; B-Level (mono and stereo) is equivalent to the very best FM radio broadcasts, transmitted and received under optimum conditions; and C-Level (mono and stereo) is equivalent to AM radio transmitted and received under optimum conditions.

16 channels each of 72 minutes' duration are available to play back the audio. A-level stereo uses 8 of them at once, so, allowing for some computer control data as well, a CD-I disc can contain just over 2 hours

A-level stereo if there is nothing else on the disc; on the other hand, a disc full of C-level mono (using one channel at a time) and containing nothing else could produce a talking book over 16 hours long - or one program in 16 different languages.

In the critical trade-off between space and quality, A-Level stereo is best reserved for a musical interlude, while C-Level is used for commentary or background music when other data need a good share of the available resources.

CD-I VIDEO

CD-I also offers a choice of video picture quality: normal resolution for most video pictures; double resolution, for better definition of computer text and graphics; and high resolution, to meet future standards in digital television.

CD-I defines four main types of full-colour picture, and a choice of techniques to record and process these as economically as possible.

- 'Natural' images such as photographic still frames use a video-based technique called DYUV, which offers very subtle and realistic color and shading.

- Computer text and graphics can use RGB (Red, Green, Blue) computer coding, but more often use a Color Look-up Table (CLUT), which creates a palate of up to 256 colors at a time.

- Simple cartoon style drawings use Run-length coding for large blocks of single colour. These simple images can be processed quickly enough to create animation on the screen.

Where conventional video creates and records special effects when the master tape is edited, CD-I can simulate many effects from still pictures recorded on the disc. These include:

- cuts, wipes, fades and dissolves between images;

- mosaics and granulation;

- scrolling horizontally or vertically;

- partial updates which change the picture in only part of the screen.

These can be achieved through the use of CD-I's four visual planes: a small 'cursor' plane at the front of the screen, two full-screen planes and a background plane for a fixed backdrop. A variety of images can be created by building up a composite picture using two or more of these planes simultaneously. Clearly, there are considerable opportunities for the creative designer.

THE DESIGN PROCESS

In the early stages at least, it is likely that most CD-I projects will be based on successful work in other media, where the familiarity of the concept or title will attract consumers unfamiliar with the new technology.

Work may well begin with documents such as the client's brief, the design company's proposal, and the treatment and contract documents then worked out between the two.

Essential production documents will likely include a storyboard, a flowchart, and scripts for both narration and text screens. The storyboard illustrates both the appearance of the finished presentation and the interactivity mapped out in the flowchart. In CD-I as in interactive video, creative energy is concentrated at this stage, and not inproduction, for the scale and complexity of the job means that every detail must be agreed before the functional work of creating and assembling the component parts begins.

Many things may happen in parallel during the assembly stage: shooting original pictures, creating graphics and text screens, recording soundtracks, preparing computer programming and so on.

When all the material is brought together, it is encoded and compressed to create data files for testing on a simulator (a large computer with hard disc storage). Here it must be rigorously tested and evaluated, and adjustments made until all the interactive elements work smoothly together. Only then is it prepared for digital encoding and pressing as a compact disc.

Even then, the work of implementation and evaluation may continue for months or years, particularly in so new a medium, to learn from the users' responses what people really want and expect from this exciting new medium.

This chapter has given an overview of the family of optical recording technologies and a short description of the salient features of CD-I. The following chapters will build on the brief look into CD-I that was presented here to include descriptions of the full range of media options and the stages in the process of designing a CD-I title.

CHAPTER 3: WHAT CD-I CAN DO

The last chapter provided a broad overview of the background to the development of optical disc technologies and briefly described the features and capabilities of CD-I. This chapter looks at the wide ranging media palette available to the CD-I designer. Specific reference is made to the audio-visual concepts behind CD-I technology. More details of how CD-I provides these capabilities, in technical terms, are found in Chapter 7.

USING AN INTERACTIVE TELEVISION SET

The heart of CD-I lies in its name - interactivity: CD-I's ability to search and locate the information requested by the user as whenever it is required. Also, CD-I can present this information in combinations of photographs, cartoons, music, speech and text, all of which can be called up at will by the user.

CD-I is aimed primarily at consumers. It will also be extremely attractive to the professional and electronic publishing markets for such topics as education and training, catalog shopping and travel information.

CD-I has the great advantage of being able to do many of the things that other optical disc products can do, but at the same time offering many other features as well. It will both play super hi-fi music from CD-Audio discs and also display the massive amounts of text and graphics typically stored on CD-ROM discs. In addition, CD-I has been designed to meet consumers' expectations of high quality video in still and moving pictures, photographs, cartoons and computer graphics.

The enormous repertoire apparent to the consumer is backed up by technical features which the designer must master in order to take full advantage of the opportunities presented by CD-I.

CD-I will play back in all current television standards and, through its interactive features, allow the user to pick and choose, mix and match. It also offers an enormous range of special effects and technical features. In addition to those commonly available in existing audio visual media like a choice of mono or stereo sound, video wipes and fades, and 3-D graphic images, CD-I also offers, in real-time, a choice of still or motion video, three different audio levels, three degrees of picture resolution, four coding techniques, and four separate image planes with and without transparency.

The description of these features presented in this chapter should give the designer sufficient background to sketch out the concept of a CD-I project. More detailed technical information is available in later chapters.

AN EXAMPLE: CD-I GOLF

The golf game described in the opening of the previous chapter makes use of the wide ranging options of a CD-I system.

A game of armchair golf combines the thrill and expertise of an arcade-style game with the high quality sound and visual images we expect from television.

The control device attached to the system - a specially designed remote control unit, a mouse, a joystick or perhaps a full computer keyboard on some - allows interaction with the animated character. Moving the cursor to the golfer's hat, allows the whole body to move on the screen, aligning the direction of the shot. Moving the cursor to the ball, controls the swing. Holding down a switch or button starts the backswing, releasing the switch releases the forward swing and tapping once again determines the moment of impact with the ball. The resulting flight of the ball has been determined by the skill of the player.

With CD-I, you don't simply jump into a swing-and-hit game. CD-I golf is a multi-media experience. Earlier, we chose the Augusta National course in Georgia. Before we started play, we finished the hotdog and coke, while watching a documentary about the course.

It was no different than watching a program on television. It showed us top quality photographic views of the course, aerial views of the hole layouts, even illustrated maps of the course with inset video sequences showing the great comeback victory of Jack Nicklaus at the Master's in 1986. And the sound - marvellous! Narration, background music, even sound effects that were almost as pure and clear as listening to music without pictures from a CD audio disc which we could put on the same player.

Many of the effects that make CD-I programs a delight to watch and listen to, or even control and interact with, are created within the CD-I system itself. Whether you are planning a golf game, devising a tour through a museum, designing a language learning course or a music survey disc, understanding and using these features opens up a vast range of program possibilities for the CD-I designer.

AUDIO

CD-I audio can be played back through a home hi-fi system as well as through a domestic television set. It therefore not only meets existing hi-fi audio expectations, but also offers hi-fi audio in combination with high quality video images.

Quality Levels and Capacity

CD-Digital Audio (CD-DA) can store just over an hour's worth of stereo sound of the highest quality on a single 12cm disc - but it devotes the whole of the compact disc's storage and processing capacity to this end.

Whilst CD-I can of course play back CD-DA quality audio, space has to be made available, both on the disc and in the processing channels, for the other media - natural video images, graphics and text. The system offers the designer three quality levels of audio in mono and stereo.

The higher the quality level, the more data has to be stored and, at the appropriate moment, transferred from the disc. Therefore, the choice of quality level can be critical for some titles. It must be determined by the disc designer according the needs of his design, the disc capacity, and the space available in the data channel.

On many occasions, there will have to be a trade-off of quality level against transfer rate or disc capacity. It is therefore important that the designer understands from the outset the difference among the quality levels.

These audio levels are:

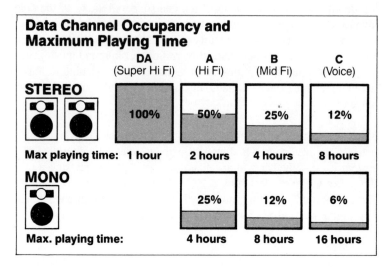

Data Channel Occupancy and Maximum Playing Time

	DA (Super Hi Fi)	A (Hi Fi)	B (Mid Fi)	C (Voice)
STEREO	100%	50%	25%	12%
Max playing time:	1 hour	2 hours	4 hours	8 hours
MONO		25%	12%	6%
Max. playing time:		4 hours	8 hours	16 hours

- A-Level audio, equivalent to the first play of a brand-new high-quality audio LP, but, because it is read by a laser beam, without any of the noise commonly created by contact between needle and disc. Stereo audio of this quality requires only half as much information as CD-DA, and thus occupies only 50% of the data channel, leaving the remaining 50% available to handle other material (video, graphics and text). Mono A-level audio occupies only 25% of the data channel.

If the whole of the disc were to be filled with A-Level audio and nothing else, just over two hours' pure stereo (or four hours of mono), could be recorded on a single disc.

- B-Level audio, equivalent to the very best stereo FM radio broadcasts, transmitted and received under the very best conditions. Stereo audio of this quality requires only 25% of the data channel and so leaves the remaining 75% of the data channel available for other material.

If the whole disc were to be filled with B-Level audio, over four hours' stereo or eight hours' mono music could be stored.

- C-Level audio is equivalent to AM radio when broadcast and received under optimum conditions. Audio of this quality in mono occupies only 6% of the data channel, leaving 94% for other material.

If the whole disc were to be filled with C-Level mono audio, over 16 hours audio could be played back.

Where CD-DA handles a single channel providing up to 72 minutes of stereo sound, CD-I offers up to 16 channels in mono. Sound can be played continuously as music or narration.

In addition sound can be transferred from the disc to the player and stored as soundmaps in the CD-I system short-term memory to respond to interactive cues from the user.

The wide range of potential applications for CD-I will require a variety of audio effects from high-quality stereo music to mono voice-overs and narrations. The contribution made by the audio track at any one moment will help determine what quality level (and so, disc and channel space) it merits: this may vary from segment to segment within the program as attention shifts between audio, video, text screens and pure interaction.

In a music video, it may be worth spending up to half the available disc resources for high-quality sound; in a multi-lingual production, the multiple parallel tracks can be used for example to provide over an hour's narration in 16 different languages - and allow the user to switch between these at will.

Soundmaps

In addition to taking the sound directly from the disc, short sound sequences can be stored in the player's own temporary memory for ready access and processing without further reference to the disc. These sequences are known within the CD-I specification as 'soundmaps'.

Typically, a soundmap might be used where a short sound effect may be repeated quite often during the course of a segment or program, e.g. in response to a user's interaction. Once the soundmap is stored in the decoder's RAM memory, it can be called up at any time, while the player itself retrieves information of other kinds from other areas of the disc.

Chapter 6: Hot Shot Sports: Audio

Chapter 5: Basic Principles: System RAM

Soundmaps may be mono or stereo and at any quality level. Two mono soundmaps may be mixed to achieve one stereo soundmap, or sound data from the disc may be mixed with a soundmap to produce another soundmap altogether. Soundmaps may be used once or looped back as often as they are needed.

Soundmaps may also be used to improve the performance of a CD-I program by providing temporary storage. Sound can be pre-loaded from the disc at a convenient moment into one soundmap into order to release the whole of the data channel at a later moment for other material; or to be mixed and played back with the output from another part of the disc.

Specialist Use

In addition to playback of stored sound, the CD-I system microprocessor can be used to generate its own sound. Specialist titles such as computer music applications could come provided with optional hardware such as a synthesizer keyboard to be attached to the system.

Audio Control

The stereo audio output levels may be controlled in a number of ways including, for example, panning from right to left, or attenuating under the control of the application on the disc.

VIDEO

CD-I has been designed to meet consumers' expectations of the highest quality video in still and moving pictures, photographs and computer graphics. CD-I shares many features with other audio-visual media - particularly, specialeffects such as cuts, wipes, dissolves and so forth. However, whereas in conventional video production, these effects can be created and recorded only in the editing suite, CD-I can also create effects within the player itself.

It also has a unique combination of additional video features to offer the designer - playback on all international television standards, a choice of image resolutions, as well as access to four video planes.

National TV Broadcast Standards

CD-I will play back on all television broadcast standards. Currently, there are two main (incompatible) broadcast television standards used variously throughout the world, each with different screen display sizes. The system used in North America and Japan employs a 525-line screen updated at 30 times per second. This is known as NTSC. The PAL system is used in Britain, most of Europe, Australia, Africa and South America is based on a 625-line screen. A full picture is updated 25 times per second.

CD-I overcomes this problem of incompatibility. A disc which has been made to the CD-I standard for international use could be bought in New York and played on a machine in London, Leningrad or Bombay - just as for CD music discs.

Resolution

CD-I provides three levels of video resolution just as it offers three levels of audio quality:

- Normal resolution is equivalent to the best picture quality obtainable on a normal broadcast television receiver; it is likely that most CD-I images will appear in normal resolution.

- Double resolution is equivalent to the best picture quality obtainable on a standard computer color monitor, and provides better reproduction of high-quality computer text and graphics.

- High resolution is equivalent to the best quality digital picture generated in the studio to AES/EBU standards.

These resolutions can best be expressed in terms of the number of picture elements (known as pixels) which appear across the screen both horizontally and vertically.

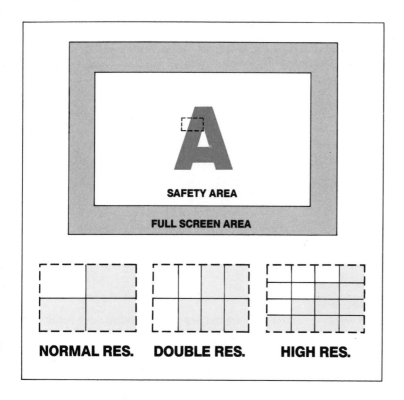

Safety Area

The video picture tends to drift beyond the edge of the visible screen, particularly in older sets. This is known as overscan. Because of this, both television systems define a safety area in normal resolution 320 pixels across, which is 210 rows high in 525-line systems (NTSC), and 250 rows high in 625-line systems (PAL/SECAM). In broadcasting this is known as the television safe title zone, and is virtually guaranteed to display adequately on all television receivers. When designing for international compatibility the CD-I designer should keep important information within adisplay area of 210 rows of 320 pixels (normal resolution).

Screen Resolution in Pixels

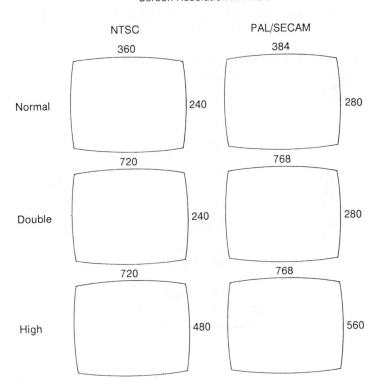

Compression
CD-I employs compression techniques to store and retrieve audio data as efficiently as possible. A variety of techniques are also used in picture coding to minimize the sometimes considerable demands of high-quality visuals.

Where conventionally-coded RGB graphics (Red, Green, Blue - the standard computer graphic coding system) might occupy 300k bytes of digital storage space and take nearly two seconds to load, compression techniques reduce this to around 100k bytes, loadable in less than a second.

Coding Techniques

Four coding techniques are available to the designer. One, known as DYUV, is best suited to photographic images. Two, RGB 5:5:5 and CLUT are more appropriate for text and complex graphics. While, finally, Run-length coding is available for text, cartoons and graphics which use large blocks of color.

Natural photographic images are best handled through a compression technique known as DYUV, or Differential (or Delta) YUV coding. This is based on conventional broadcast television and video technology, where Y represents the luminance of a video signal, and U and V its color. A combination of coding techniques based on compressing the color signals, and coding only differences between consecutive pixels results in a compression ratio of 3:1 in comparison with conventional RGB coding.

Chapter 5: Disc Capacity

When subtle shades and gradual changes in tone and texture are required, such as in photographic images, DYUV is ideal. It is not suitable for text and those graphics which call for a crisper and less subtle display.

Chapter 7: DYUV Images

In cases where high resolution is needed for a natural image, a technique known as QHY (Quantized High-resolution Y) can enhance the luminance ('Y') signal to achieve this (the color resolution is sufficient already). Instead of direct high resolution DYUV coding, which would require four times the disc and memory space, high resolution is achieved by interpolation. QHY is used to correct the interpolated values where these differ significantly from the true values. This feature is not in the Base Case hardware specification.

Three coding methods are available for graphics: RGB 5:5:5, CLUT and Run-length coding.

RGB 5:5:5 is available only in normal resolution, and provides a compression ratio of 1.5:1 - that is, around 200k bytes per full screen image - by reducing the number of RGB levels from 256 to 32 (or 8-bits to 5-bits) per RGB. This still leaves a range of 32,768 colors to choose from. It is very good for graphics, and best suited to user-manipulated graphics such as paint or drawing applications. Because other coding techniques are available which compress the image at a higher ratio with little loss apprarent to the user, RGB 5:5:5 is a relatively inefficient means of coding.

Chapter 7: RGB 5:5:5 Images

CLUT, stands for Color Look-Up Table. This is the location in memory where a set of colors that the designer has defined is stored. CLUT is available at both normal and double resolution. Compression - at about the same 3:1 ratio as DYUV, and double that of RGB 5:5:5 - is achieved

Chapter 7: CLUT Images

by restricting the total number of colors available for any given image to a range of 256 or fewer, pre-selected by the designer from some 16 million ultimately available. The contents of the CLUT can be defined as having 256 levels each for red, green and blue, so the total number of colors available to the designer for a single image is 256 x 256 x 256 = over 16 million. The total range of colors available is greater than for RGB 5:5:5, but the number of colors on the display at any one time is limited. Since the human eye can only discern some 5,000 to 10,000 colors in any single image, this restriction in colors only becomes a problem for highly accurate representations of natural images where subtle gradation is essential.

When used at double resolution only 16 colors are available instead of up to 256 in normal resolution.

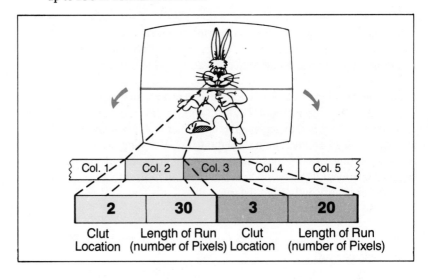

Chapter 7: Run-length Images

Run-length coding is very economical for certain types of graphic image such as cartoons which use large blocks of color. Not only are the number of different colors limited, but also the number of color changes on any one line. Images like this can be stored, retrieved and manipulated on the screen very efficiently through Run-length coding.

Run-length coding uses the CLUT to define the colors to be used. The color choice per image is limited to 128 at normal resulution and only eight colors at double resolution.

The big advantage of Run-length coding is that a typical cartoon or line drawing will require only 10k to 20k bytes of data.

It is usual to store text in a compressed form using the character coding techniques of computers. However text can also be treated as an RGB, CLUT or Run-length coded graphic image. The CD-I specification defines a standard character set covering all Latin alphabet languages, including a number of special characters for currency symbols, diacritic marks, and so forth. Alternative character sets and fonts can be created transferring information from the disc into the decoder, so CD-I is truly multi-national and multi-lingual.

Image Planes

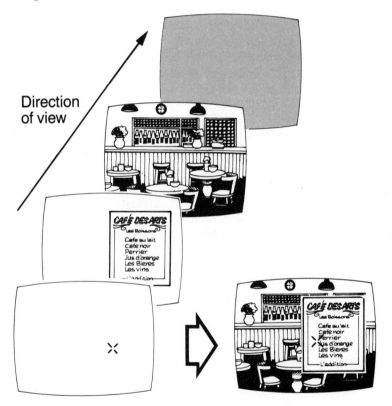

Chapter 3: Visual Effects

Chapter 5: Screen Effects

The picture which the viewer sees on the screen can be composed of several image planes which appear one behind the other. CD-I offers up to 4 image planes. The first is a limited area 16 pixel x 16 pixel single color cursor plane. Behind this can be one or two full-screen image planes,which may be coded and displayed individually or together in any combination of DYUV and CLUT.

Alternatively these two planes can be merged into one plane so that an RGB 5:5:5 image, which uses twice as much data as the other coding methods, may be displayed.

Behind these planes is a fourth or background plane (not in use in the illustration) which acts as a backdrop in cases where all or part of both image planes are transparent. The backdrop may be a single color selected from a fixed range of 16. In some CD-I players, the backdrop may be replaced by an external video source.

The experienced audio visual designer will readily appreciate the enormous potential offered by this combination of planes.

Motion

The capabilities of CD-I have so far been described in terms of still images. CD-I is not a still image medium and the designer is encouraged to use motion where it is needed. However, because of technical considerations, care must be taken in designing motion material. It is important for the designer to understand the ways in which motion is achieved.

The first technical consideration is disc capacity. In computing terms, 650 Mb of data is an enormous store. In feature movie terms, however, one would be forgiven for believing that 7,800 DYUV video images will get eaten up in about 4.5 minutes. But of course a movie does not show 7,800 totally different images in 4.5 minutes - a lingering romantic movie might show only two or three basic images in that time with quite subtle differences between most frames. So disc capacity can only be calculated with precision when the actual information load - the quantity of separate bits of information to be shown on the screen - is known. This quantity can only be measured after the coding techniques and frame rate are known. This is another example of how important it is that the designer understand the technical requirements of CD-I - that means in the first instance reading right through Chapter 7 and the Appendices. This chapter is not the place to delve into so much detail. Suffice it to say at this stage that the designer should be aware that disc capacity is a constraint, but not a great constraint, if CD-I's features are to be used to the full.

There are a number of ways in which images can be given motion when this is required.

Full motion on the screen can be achieved through partial updates - that is, a technique which changes the picture in only part of the screen at one time. The rate at which data can be transferred from the disc means that only about 13% of the screen can be updated fast enough to achieve full motion video.

However, cognitive full motion - that iswhere no subjective motion jitter or blur can be seen by 95% of the population - requires a minimum of 10 frames per second. The designer can achieve moving images at this rate covering up to 50% of the screen by using software coding techniques.

If an even larger picture area is required, full motion video can be displayed by using chroma key - a video technique frequently used on television in which one image plane of moving elements within the picture is electronically keyed over a still or scrolling image in the second plane. The size of image which can be achieve on CD-I depends, as always, on the amount of new information to be transferred from the disc.

A similar multi-plane technique is an integral feature of traditional cel animation in which the still elements of a scene are constantly re-used and a separate cel for the parts which move is laid over the top - typically at the rate of 10 to 15 frames per second. Run-length coding is a good technique to use in achieving full screen full motion animation since the typical Run-length image over the full screen may occupy between 8k and 15k bytes.

Again, the update rate will, of course, depend on the actual complexity of the images and the amount of space available for them, which in turn depends on the audio quality level and other data needed at the time.

Limited animation effects may be produced by re-defining the CLUT colors. A singalong sequence in a music application might show a ball moving across the screen to help the listener follow the words of a song. To simulate the movement of the ball as it follows the text, a series of circular shapes are laid out on the screen, which can be colored using locations in the color look-up table.

Chapter 6: Pop Showcase: Screen Proportion

The balls can be made transparent by making each one the same color as the background. By successively changing the colors to yellow and back to the background color, the ball appears to move across the screen. The CLUT contents are successively re-defined as the ball moves across the screen.

This simple technique, of course, may require a number of spare CLUT locations, but it can be very powerful.

Another possibility is dynamic CLUT update. By re-defining the CLUT from line to line down the display, the number of colors available in an image may be expanded to the limit that can be loaded into one field - about 2,000 colors.

By re-defining CLUT colors in these ways, it is possible to create a range of highly dynamic effects.

VISUAL EFFECTS

CD-I can not only store and retrieve virtually any image as a high-quality still or graphic, but the range of special effects available within the system itself includes cuts, wipes, dissolves, granulation, scrolling and animation -enough features to rival most things to be found in modern video editing suites !

Single Plane Operations

Some effects can be achieved on a single image plane, but many require both. Single plane operations include cuts, sub-screens, scrolling, mosaic effects and fading.

Cuts

The cut - the sudden change from one image to another - is the simplest visual effect. In a single plane this means cutting between images stored in the player's own temporary memory. A number of images may be held this way and used at a rate faster than any designer would likely want to use them.

Cuts can also be performed, of course, by switching directly from one plane to another.

Partial updates are rapid cuts in a single plane covering only part of the full screen image. Rapid cuts give full motion video.

Sub-screens

7-bit
CLUT

SUBSCREEN
3-bit
CLUT

Each image plane may be divided into a number of horizontal bands called sub-screens which can, if necessary, use a different coding method. So images of different kinds can be shown together without recourse to both image planes. In the example shown in the diagram, the screen is divided in three parts: the main picture can be two DYUV images and the band in the lower portion of the screen a text image using double resolution CLUT or Run-length coding. The number of sub-screens, their positions and their boundaries formed by horizontal lines may be defined by the designer at will - in the extreme, each of the 525 or 625 lines could be a sub-screen. The advantage of using this technique in the instance illustrated (a pattern recognition game for under 5s) is that it frees the other visual plane for a larger, more visible cursor.

Chapter 6: Interactive
Under Fives

Scrolling

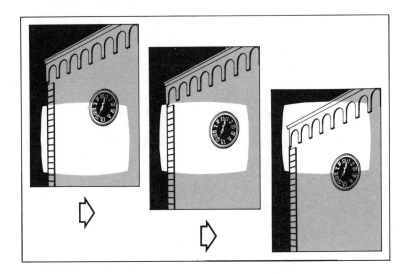

Images may be scrolled horizontally or vertically. Simple examples include the vertical scroll of a picture of a clocktower from the base towards the top, or a horizontal scroll across an image stored in memory, perhaps a panoramic view much wider than the screen itself. In either case, the screen acts as a window onto the larger image. The relative positions of the image and the screen can be changed to facilitate smooth scrolling at any speed.

A combination of sub-screens and scrolling allows a central area to be scrolled between two fixed areas of the screen at top and bottom.

Mosaic Effects

Mosaic effects can be used for granulation and magnification of an image; basically, they involve reducing the resolution of the image through one of two mechanisms called pixel hold and pixel repeat. Partial updates of reduced resolution images covering a larger part of the screen can be achieved in this way.

Pixel hold retains the whole picture but reduces the resolution by making the image appear granulated. This is achieved by taking a pixel value and holding onto it for a defined number of pixel positions both horizontally and vertically. The different value (or colour) of the other pixels in the original image is ignored. This technique can be used with any image coding method, including DYUV and Run-length; the hold factor can be any number from 1 to 255, which may be independently set for horizontal and vertical directions.

Pixel hold is used for granulation effects where the size of an image remains constant, but a blocking effect is produced as shown in the figure. In this example, with a hold factor of two in each direction, every other pixel in both horizontal and vertical directions is expanded to four pixels on the screen, although the total image size remains the same. By changing the hold factor, the resolution of an image can gradually be reduced until it becomes unrecognizable, at which point, the image can be cut to another and the hold factor gradually reduced so that the new image now appears.

Pixel repeat magnifies a portion of the image without providing greater detail. Each pixel is displayed a number of times in sequence, as shown in the figure. A pixel can only be repeated 2, 4, 8 or 16 times. This technique can only be used with CLUT and RGB 5:5:5 coding so pixel repeat can be used for reduced resolution images, which require less data from the disc, or to magnify or zoom images.

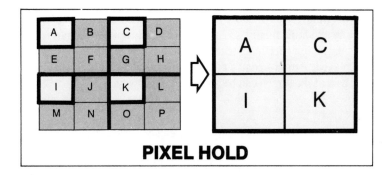

PIXEL HOLD

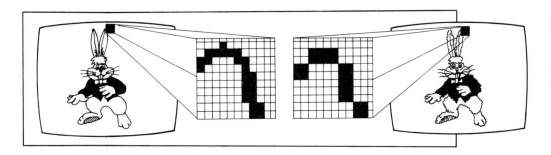

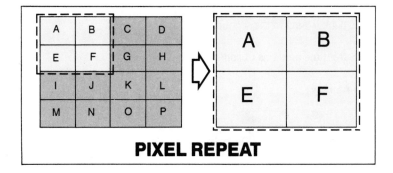

PIXEL REPEAT

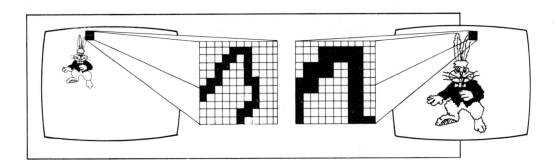

In the diagram, a part of one image is magnified by a factor of two both vertically and horizontally, so each pixel in the original becomes four in the displayed image. Unlike pixel hold, only a part of the total image can be displayed. Partial updates of reduced resolution images covering a larger part of the screen can be achieved in this way.

Fade

The brightness or intensity of any image can be varied from black to full intensity through a range of 64 levels. Different parts of an image can be given different levels of brightness than other parts, so only parts of an image fade. It is more likely that this effect will be used to move from one image to the next in combination with two-plane effects.

Two-Plane Effects

All of the coding methods except RGB 5:5:5 allow for two separate image planes. The use of two planes, together with transparency, can provide a range of very useful effects including transparency in parts of an image, mixing of images, dissolves and wipes.

Transparency

The most obvious reason for providing transparency is so that the second image plane, or part of it, can be viewed through the first image plane. For example, a cartoon image in the first plane can be placed over a fixed scenic background in the second plane.

There are three methods of achieving transparency.

Chroma Key

Chapter 6: French
Phrasebook

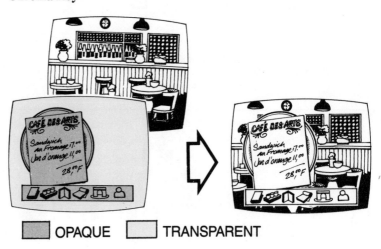

■ OPAQUE   □ TRANSPARENT

The first is the use of chroma key or color key, a technique which has been used in the video industry for many years. Red, Green and Blue, the RGB colors, for each pixel are compared to the color key value, which is defined in 8 bits of red, green and blue.

If the pixel color and the key color match, then that pixel is made transparent revealing the background. Since the color key function operates on the final RGB values, it is independent of the coding method.

Mattes

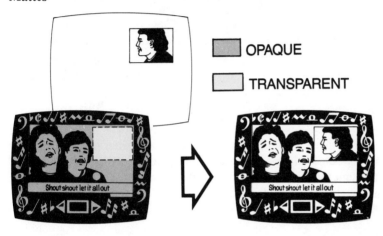

A second method for achieving transparency is the use of mattes. A matte is an area of any shape - regular or irregular - which is defined on the screen so that the area inside the matte is transparent and the area outside is not.

This is achieved independently of color key or any other transparency mechanism. A number of mattes can appear on the screen at one time and two mattes can overlap.

Transparent Pixels

In RGB 5:5:5 only, there is a transparency bit available for each pixel, so any combination of pixels can be made transparent.

Since RGB 5:5:5 does not allow the use of two planes, only the backdrop or external video can be seen when the transparency bit is used.

Dissolves

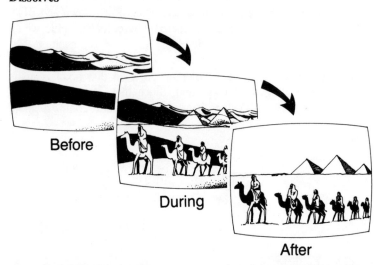

Before

During

After

As explained, it is possible to adjust the intensity of an image. By mixing the two image planes together at different intensities then translucency can be achieved. One example of this is the dissolve, where one image can turn into another by changing the intensity for each image so that one increases as the other decreases, and so one apprear to dissolve into the other.

The use of mattes allows mixing and dissolving to be restricted to parts of the screen defined by those mattes.

Wipes

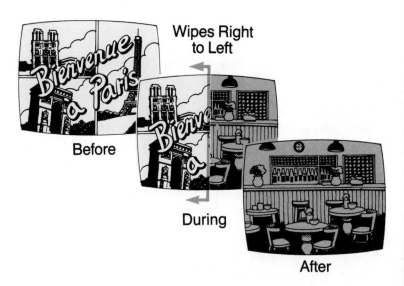

Wipes Right
to Left

Before

During

After

This is another way to change from one image to another which requires two planes. For example the figure shows a horizontal wipe, where one image changes into another by a wipe from from right to left. This can be achieved quite simply through the use of mattes where a simple rectangular matte, for example, starting from the right hand side of the screen and gradually moving across to the left hand side produces a wipe. Wipes can of course be horizontal or vertical and in either direction. Mattes can, of course, have different shapes and be varied in size, so for example a diamond shaped matte can start very small and gradually increase in size until the new image covers the full screen.

REAL-TIME INTERACTIVITY

This chapter has so far discussed the audio-visual elements in CD-I, but another essential feature is of courseinteractivity. Digital data on CD-I discs may contain audio, video, text or graphics. Data can also be used to control the presentation itself and to interact with the user in front of the screen. All this must happen in 'real-time' (rather than, say the artificially fast or slow speeds common in computing), which makes special demands on CD-I technology.

Real-time Data
Audio and video are of course played from the disc in real-time. In addition, data of any kind from any part of the disc can be accessed - that is, found and retrieved - at random. This access is instantaneous if the new data is close by, and no longer than two seconds if the laser has to travel from one extreme position to another.

CD-I decoders can handle a variety of tasks in parallel and in real-time: this is essential if audio, video, text and graphics are to be synchronized to reach the user in the right order and at the right time.

Synchronization
Synchronization is very critical in the kind of complex multi-media presentation that CD-I offers. In the example shown here, the visual of the golf club swing must synchronize with a carefully-timed audio effect as the club hits the ball. The timing of the synchronization cue depends upon the instant that the player - acting through a remote control or other input device - determines, which in turn designates the exact moment of contact of the club on the ball.

Chapter 5:
Microprocessor

Chapter 5:
Synchronizing to Video

This sound effect can be handled as a sound map pre-stored in RAM and played through the audio output channels at the required moment. The basic images are taken from disc and stored in RAM as drawmaps, and the animation sequences are handled by manipulation of the appropriate drawmaps.

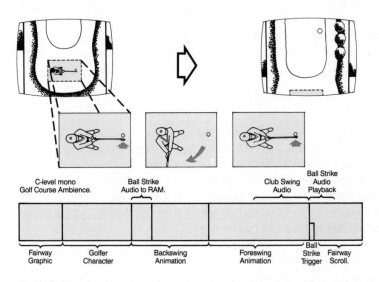

Synchronization is controlled through data recorded on disc, and may occur in response to pre-recorded 'triggers' in the program, or the user's spontaneous response to the program. These elements of the technology are explained more fully in Chapter 7.

USER INTERFACES

Interaction would be impossible without suitable user interfaces - that is, devices which allow the user to control or react to information on the screen by making choices, decisions and requests. An important element of the CD-I design task lies in the preparation of these essential user interfaces.

Physical Interface

The CD-I system specifies an X-Y pointing device as the main user interface. This could be a keypad, a mouse, a joystick, a light pen, a graphics tablet. It is always equipped with two trigger buttons which may be used in a variety of ways determined by the designer.

The specific device chosen may depend on the application or range of applications used, and individual CD-I players may well allow a choice. For example, a mouse is suitable when sitting at a table close up to the screen for making selections or doing simple drawings on the screen. An infra red keypad would be most appropriate for those listening to and watching a disc in television mode - from the other side of the room.

Appendix C: The Pointing Device

Chapter 6: Interactive Under Fives

As an option, an alphanumeric keyboard may be provided with CD-I players. This will be necessary where the user is required to input long or complex textual responses.

For players which do not have a QWERTY keyboard, a simplified keyboard can be displayed on the screen and the X-Y pointer used to select characters from it.

Interacting with the User

A pointing device may be used to move the cursor around the screen. By controlling the cursor position, the user can select menu items or buttons, move level controls and so forth. Scrolling around an image which is larger than the display screen may be achieved through directional arrows or sliders on the screen.

The screen may therefore be designed to include certain areas, such as buttons - also known as hot spots or action areas. These allow the user to make selections, go back to a main menu or pause within an application. They may be displayed explicitly on the screen so that the user can see them, or the designer of a game for example may have decided that they should be invisible.

Interaction with the user is an essential part of a CD-I system and the designer must take great care to ensure that the display on the screen is always clear and designed in such a way as to make it inviting. The user must always understand readilty what to do - and, indeed, what can be done at any point in the programme.

CONCLUSION

This chapter has shown the range of features available to the CD-I designer. The combinations into which these may be woven may at times be bewildering, and certainly make the design process much more complex than that for any other audio visual medium. However, rich rewards await the imaginative designer who can master the techniques and who can conceive and develop programs that will set the world new standards of creative achievement.

CHAPTER 4: THE DESIGN BRIEF

Chapter 3 surveyed the media palette available to the CD-I designer. This chapter looks at the special creative and technical challenges posed to the designer by CD-I, and suggests some pertinent questions for the would-be producer to consider. It outlines typical stages in the design and production of a CD-I project, and discusses the skills and backgrounds required of members of the design team.

The previous chapter showed the wide variety of sound and picture making effects incorporated into the CD-I system. It is evident that a high level of planning and control is necessary if truly exciting and intellectually rewarding programs are to be created.

Like all successful publications of high quality, CD-I discs must be designed on the basis of a very clear understanding of the user and particularly what the user wants or expects from the program and the technology. So the very first task for the designer to address is not how to exploit the exciting opportunities that the technology offers but, rather, the age old issues of who will want the product, how it will fit into the market place, and what attributes of the subject matter make it suitable for the medium.

The successful designer is one who can answer these questions accurately, and as a result develop a product that will interest and excite the audience. CD audio has established the compact disc as a quality product in the minds of the public. CD-I must build on that reputation and success. It is therefore important that the first discs meet consumers' expectations of a product which is new, and unlike anything else on the market: informative, entertaining, worth the money, and yet not too frighteningly modern or complex - in fact, somehow familiar.

DEVELOPING THE DESIGN BRIEF

To develop a clear design brief, the potential CD-I designer will need first to address several key questions:

- Why choose this title ? Is it best suited to the market opportunities of CD-I?

- How does this title fit in with the others already on the market? Does it duplicate, complement or supercede existing products?

- Who will want to buy the disc? - especially if they have to buy a CD-I player, too

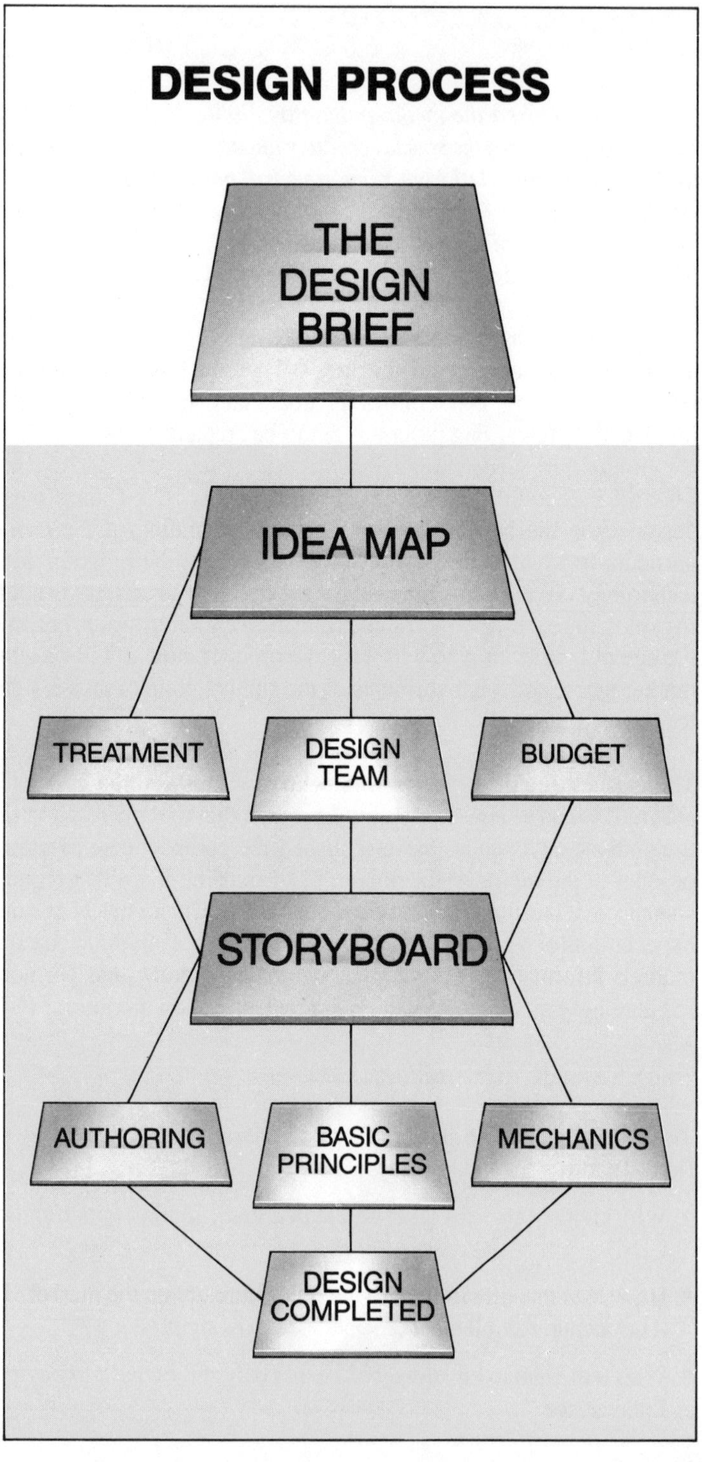

DESIGN PROCESS

THE
DESIGN
BRIEF

IDEA MAP

TREATMENT

DESIGN
TEAM

BUDGET

STORYBOARD

AUTHORING

BASIC
PRINCIPLES

MECHANICS

DESIGN
COMPLETED

- How will the interactivity be used? How will the program retain its interest over many playing sessions? What will happen if the program is left unattended or the user is unable to respond?

As CD-I grows, the industry will be able to address these and other questions in more detail. However, the experience of other media - including interactive video - offers some guidance.

Why choose this title? Is it best suited to the market opportunities of CD-I?

CD-I can combine high quality photographic images, full-color graphics, animation, text and sound in a range of qualities and presented in new and potentially exciting ways - and it can store huge volumes of this information, compactly in digital form on a single small disc: this we know.

The CD-I designer must decide whether any of these features adds real value to a product which could be made in another, more conventional, medium. The CD-I title must use CD-I's unique attributes appropriately - and be readily accessible to the consumer. The temptation to exploit the technology simply because it's there, or seek novelty for its own sake must be firmly resisted!

Particularly in the early years, adaptations from other successful mass market publications - books, video or computer software - will be important. People unsure of the technology will respond to a familiar title or concept, and this will form a bridge from the new product to established markets. However, to capture these new sales, it is important that CD-I really does add new dimensions to a product already successful in another medium. Otherwise, why buy the CD-I version?

The creation of a totally original concept for CD-I will present the greatest challenge to the CD-I designer - but the reward will be a purpose-built product which makes full use of the CD-I's unique potential, in creatively imaginative ways.

A series of titles which make use of use the same basic design and production processes will help to diffuse the work and cost of developing software for the new medium. Typically these might include games, instructional materials, reference works and entertainment such as pop music programs or children's shows.

Ask:

- Is this a commercial, promotable, consumer product?

- What does CD-I technology contribute?

- If it is an adaptation from another medium, what is the audience profile and sales history of that medium? How does that compare to the immediate prospects for CD-I, outlined below?

How does this title fit in with the others already on the market? Does it duplicate, complement or supercede existing products?

The first CD-I designers will waste effort if they try to produce a title which is already in production elsewhere, or does not fit into the range of products already indevelopment. There is simply not the room for two similar titles in such a new market.

Content providers, those who own titles already successful in other media, will look to CD-I as a means of re-exploiting the market. Fears that the new medium will destroy the market for the old product are ill-founded.

It has been established, for example, that the film of the book and the book of the film stimulate demand for each other.

The Grolier Multi-media Encyclopedia - one of many titles currently in production - is not a more conveniently shaped and packaged clone of the 20-volume print Academic American Encyclopedia, but an entirely different and complementary product providing education, information and entertainment in ways not previously envisaged.

Ask:

- Do I know enough about other titles that are being produced? Where can I learn more - from the publishing and AV trade press? From professional associations and groups? From the grapevine?

Who will want to buy the disc? - especially if they have to buy a CD-I player, too?

The first CD-I players will be sold in the United States and will cost in the region of $1500. Multi-media controllers to adapt many of the recently manufactured CD Audio players to take CD-I discs will cost about $1000. So it can be assumed that, like the first motor cars, televisions and CD Audio players, CD-I players and titles will sell first to audiences who welcome innovation.

They are consumers who:

- like electronics for home entertainment (stereo, video, computers);

- own a CD Audio player;

- are willing to buy a new kind of software, even when there are relatively few titles available;

- are less sensitive to price than most;

- like to be the 'first on the block' with any new product or status symbol.

Each potential CD-I project must be thoroughly analysed for its commercial potential in that market. Likely applications will include education and information, but entertainment is expected to lead the market.

The true multi-media nature of CD-I will allow designers to draw on the very best of published material and titles will not be limited to the types of electronic material currently available for home computers and in arcades.

Chapter 6: Typical CD-I Applications

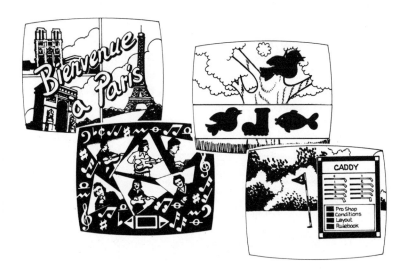

Typical applications might include armchair travel and language courses with authentic sounds and pictures supported by masses of text; music tuition or a pop video that contains information and pictures as well as top-quality digital soundtracks, or even the Japanese 'karaoke' option to switch off selected voices or instruments and supply the track yourself!

Simple special effects and control commands could allow users to create original programming from the sound, pictures and text on the disc.

The initial target audience appreciates a product with educational value. CD-I can offer a constructive alternative to commercial television, and even something which encourages people of different ages to play or study together.

CD-I should prove a popular medium with children, with entertainment that is engaging, interactive and informative.

Ask:

- What is the demographic breakdown of potential purchasers? How does this profile compare with that of the first CD-I market?

- Would celebrity involvement, licensed characters and other familiar commercial elements widen the demographic base?

How will interactivity be used?

The core of any CD-I title is its interactivity: it is the elegance - or otherwise - of this design that makes or breaks the program.

Chapter 6: The Grolier
Multi-media
Encyclopedia

Chapter 6: Country
House Murders

The user will have to be given the maximum encouragement to interact with CD-I. It must be clear at all times what is to be done next; there must never be an occasion when the user can get lost within the program; the user must always feel in control. Of course the designer may spring a few surprises - one would expect as much in a game or similar application - but this must not be so sharp as to disorientate the user.

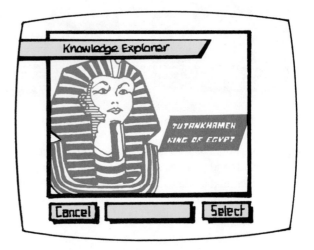

CD-I must also maintain the delicate balance between passive reception and true interaction. It is tiring to interact all the time - especially in programs which fully exploit the length and complexity permitted by CD-I's storage capacity and multiplicity of effects. Interactivity must be perceived as true added value, and not merely a gimmick which becomes annoying when the novelty wears off.

Equally, the interactions themselves must be substantial: trivial rewards could put the new user off not only that program, but the whole concept of interactive home entertainment.

A key element in this design is the input device. A CD-I base case system can support an infra red keypad - a familiar device to owners of remote control television receivers - a tracker ball, a mouse, or a joystick which may be more familiar to owners of home computers. The choice for any particular application will depend on what room the CD-I player is in and how far the viewer is from the screen, but is crucial in establishing a friendly interactive environment. Similarly, menu design and other visual aids and prompts will also play a critical role; most computer users are familiar with the technique, but others will need encouragement and guidance. For example, menus can be hidden until they are needed. They must certainly be honed until they are as clear and straightforward as possible.

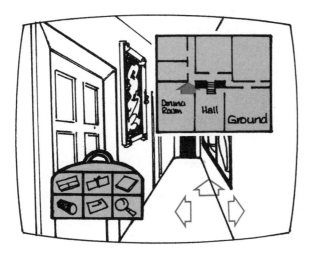

Action regions supported, for example by InVision, can be defined so that whole parts of the screen can be used to select routes through the disc: point to the door and give it a 'push' and you're inside. A whole language of icons must be devised to guide and prompt users through a range of actions and responses. Pictograms and visual aids are especially useful in multi-lingual applications, and can streamline the appearance of menus and choice frames.

Audio prompting is a very immediate and friendly way to encourage interactivity. Technophiles can be frustrated by the slowness of audio prompting, but it has worked well for general audiences in LaserVision applications, particularly in point-of-sale projects.

Paradoxically, part of the elegance of an interactive application may lie in allowing the viewer to watch some segments passively. Effective use can be made of this 'Auto-play' mode to sell the application, and to intrigue the user into trying new alternatives. It can also help the user to improve his performance by showing how the application can best be run. We do not yet know how consumers will react to interactivity at this level: what models we have - video games, for instance - are not always directly comparable with typical CD-I applications such as multi-media encyclopedias and programs to teach reading.

Ask:

- Who is going to use the title, and how?
- What is the most appropriate way of making interaction easy and fun?
- Is the user interface fit for its purpose?
- What is the right balance between interactivity and passive viewing?

DEVELOPING THE IDEA MAP

Having established the appropriateness of the title, medium and level of interactivity to the market and to the audience, the next task is for the designer to give shape to these ideas.

The design process may begin with a letter of agreement from the publisher or other 'content provider'. If the client originally submitted a brief for tender, and the production company replied with a proposal, there may now be a contract and a treatment agreed between the two.

The basic document which opens the door to pre-production will typically address the following fundamental aspects of the project.

- The Treatment,
- The Design Team
- The Budget and Schedule

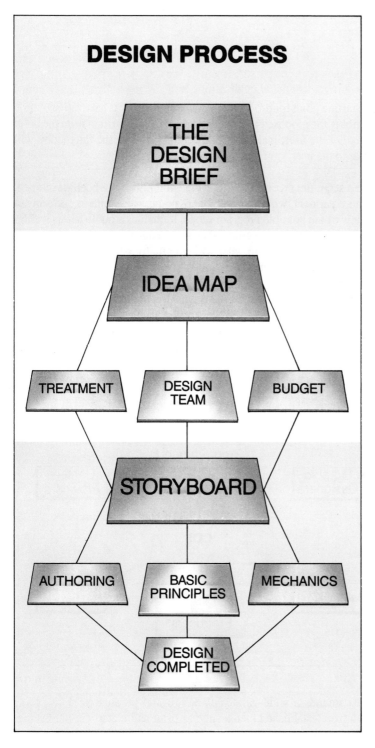

TREATMENT

The starting point for production is the treatment. It is a narrative outline describing the proposed content or storyline, often written from the point of view of the user, including a description of how the interaction will appear to the user.

At this stage the precise design of the content has not been developed, so the treatment would present a hypothetical scenario, offering a preview of the possible program scope. It enables a publisher as well as the design team to be certain that the initial project brief has been understood with regard to what will eventually be produced, mastered and bought by customers.

At a later stage of the design process this treatment may be redeveloped in a more detailed form, when the storyboard phase begins and when a clearer picture of the budget has been outlined. A detailed treatment is an essential document to brief scriptwriters and a potential source of publicity for the application.

THE DESIGN TEAM

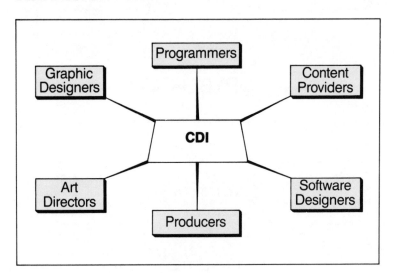

CD-I demands a wide variety of design and production skills, some drawn from established media such as print and electronic publishing, computer programming and audio-visual production, others emerging as the technology itself develops.

Yet what CD-I demands perhaps more than any other medium is not only close co-operation within the design team, but also a sound understanding by everyone involved of both the technology and the individual disciplines which make up a CD-I program. Each must understand the technology to make the best possible use of its resources; each must also understand the potential (and limits) of disciplines other than their own, to choose the best medium for each message.

In CD-I, after all, the choice between video still, computer graphic, text screen and audio is more than a creative one, when storage space and speed of transmission are at issue. The way in which the user interacts with the program is both a technical and a creative decision which affects every member of the team from the software specialist to the screen designer and the scriptwriter. For a CD-I project to be truly interactive, the whole design team must appreciate the range of technical and creative elements involved at every stage.

Chapter 5: Basic
Principles
and
The Mechanics of CD-I
Design

Thus, in CD-I, familiar job titles like 'producer', 'scriptwriter', 'graphic designer' or 'programmer' may cover a range of new and complex skills. Perhaps the early years of CD-I will offer talented and adventurous people the kind of opportunities that the early years of film-making and television did.

A Typical Design Team
- ° a project producer/director who will exercise creative control and ensure all materials are correctly integrated;
- ° a project manager who will coordinate activity and progress;
- ° a CD-I author who will control the overall interactive design and may write the script and the text screens as well;
- ° a content advisor or specialist on the content of the disc;
- ° a designer of audio-visual material and software;
- ° a graphic designer to originate images and to design user interface screens;
- ° a programmer to write the software required.

To compete on the consumer market, CD-I programs will have to offer at least as much as established favourites in television, video, hi-fi and games - which means not just excellent sound and picture quality, but also significant entertainment value and ease of use for an audience not accustomed to high levels of interaction with recorded media.

Accordingly, those with a background in film, TV or corporate video will have much to contribute to CD-I - and some new ideas to absorb and existing attitudes to change, in the shift from linear to interactive media. Yet CD-I is in many ways like a book, and the traditional skills of writers and editors as well as book designers, illustrators and art directors can profitably be transferred to CD-I. The publisher's role is similar in both media.

BUDGET AND SCHEDULE

A target production budget must be developed at the very start. Although it will be far too early to develop this in any detail, block sums can be assigned to the major elements of production. These should include the costs of the interactive design and storyboards, image, sound and text origination, This will be constantly reviewed during the initial production phase until the completion of the storyboards, when a detailed and firm budget can be fixed.

The CD-I designer must have a clear idea of the cost of the project. This might seem to be difficult to calculate, at least until a few titles of different kinds have been produced. However, many parameters exist in traditional audio visual production to enable realistic target estimates for all but the final pre-mastering phases to be developed.

However, a thorough understanding of the technology is essential to create a design which can be realized with the money available. For example, the use of CD-I's multiple soundtracks and image planes means that a single disc can be designed for a wide international market, but the additional cost of translating all the text and recording all the audio tracks must not be forgotten.

Nonetheless, once the parameters of the content, budget and the production schedule have been fixed, many elements of the project are as predictable as those of any electronic video program: salary costs can be calculated once it has been decided how many people will be involved and for how long, material resources from office space to technical facilities are predictable, as are the replication costs of the discs themselves - all familiar elements of any audio visual or publishing project to which firm estimates can be fixed.

There has currently been so little experience in CD-I production that it is not useful at this stage to assign outline costs to production. Many of the early projects being developed have budgets in the range $250,000 to $750,000, with adaptations of existing products that cost much less and large, prestige productions developed from scratch that cost a great deal more. It seems reasonable to expect budgets to be higher than single volume books, but much lower than low budget movies.

It is worth remembering that successful international book publishing ventures have made good profits on budgets well below and sometimes well in excess of these sums. Yet the potential returns from sales in a truly international market place (once it has fully developed) are likely to match the most successful books and movies.

In addition to the budget, a schedule of work, together with information on how that work is to be monitored and achieved has to be agreed.

Again, it is too early to be helpful about the length of design and production time. Simple conversions of existing interactive LaserVision products which did not seek to exploit CD-I's unique features could be completed in weeks, while a high original, bespoke product - an intricate tour of one of the world's great art galleries for example - might take years.

Whatever its length, the schedule must show, at specific critical points, where and how the review process will take place - who will be involved, and what issues are to be addressed at any particular time. Review periods may occur at fixed intervals (monthly or weekly, for example) or at the end of pre-determined production phases.

The initial project documents at the treatment stage are likely to set the terms for critical stages in the evaluation - say, completion of storyboards, during simulation, on delivery to the client, and after the program has begun to be used by its intended audience under real working conditions. In such a new medium, though, it is entirely possible that these criteria may be revised as the project develops.

The Production Process
In order to estimate the schedule of work and ultimately a projection of the cost of production, it is essential to have a clear sense of the phases that a typical application would go through as it passes from the idea stage through the design stages to eventual realization as a program on compact disc.

PHASE ONE: is the Idea Map - the development of a treatment, budget and schedule. It will also identify members of the design team and the probable outside content sources, facilities and studios that may be used in the production phase.

PHASE TWO: is concerned with the development of prototype storyboards and flowcharts. These will define the range of problems that need to be solved before production can begin and typically consist of archetypal frames, stored in electronic form or as hard copy.

Prototype storyboards will show:
- ° screen design issues
- ° elements of the user interface
- ° a list of resources for sound and pictures
- ° an outline of coding proposals and other authoring issues.

The prototype flowchart will show:
- ° the overall design for the interactive application, in both micro and macro terms
- ° any design issues which may affect the preparation of application software.

PHASE THREE: At this stage, problems are solved and definitive designs take shape. Electronic storyboards will present prototype frames, using master material for both sound and pictures. This material will later be encoded to the CD-I specification. The user interface will be comprehensively defined and the interactive flowchart will be finalized.

PHASE FOUR: Electronic storyboards can now simulate parts of the program. And the design and production parameters can be tested, using the most appropriate hardware.

PHASE FIVE: The shooting script will now contain a comprehensive list of audio-visual requirements, including how these are to be arranged. All the picture requirements will be listed according to their original format, and their encoding mode, and all audio elements will of course also be included.

A detailed budget and production schedule with reviews and income and expenditure schedules should be ready by this stage. A database management system will help to monitor all the individual production elements comprehensively throughout the project.

PHASE SIX: Production proper can now begin. After the video data has been 'captured' (whether assembled from existing material or freshly shot, or a combination of the two), it must be processed and integrated. The video images are composed and reviewed, the predetermined coding is applied, and design personnel review the data which is then entered into the database monitoring system.

PHASE SEVEN: The audio data is composed, edited, and mixed down, and the appropriate sound levels are selected. The audio material is then reviewed in the same manner as the video data.

PHASE EIGHT: Finally, authoring - the creation of the control code - is undertaken when the design is fully implemented. All the audio-visual components are linked together with all text and user inputs.

The project is now ready to be reviewed and evaluated.

CONCLUSION

The development of the Idea Map provides a broad picture of the CD-I project into the design and production phases that stretch ahead. It sets up the control procedures that will help to maintain the continuity of the work that may be carried out on several fronts at the same time. With a well laid out document, the actual process of designing a CD-I application can begin with confidence that it can and will be realized.

The mechanical design tools essential to the coordination of a CD-I application will be covered in the next chapter. These include the nature of the CD-I authoring environment, some basic principles of data management unique to CD-I, and the way in which various effects can be combined.

CHAPTER 5: DESIGNING FOR PRODUCTION

Chapter 4 looked at the early stages of the design process, in which a general plan for the development of a CD-I project is outlined. This chapter will look into the next stage, in which the design enters a more detailed phase - that of storyboard development. The chapter will outline the proposed systems that will make up the authoring environment and looks at some basic principles of CD-I design and the way in which elements are brought together in the CD-I system to produce a program that attracts and holds a user.

DEVELOPING THE STORYBOARD

Once the first stage of the design process, dealt with in the previous chapter - the treatment, budget and schedule, and the design team - have been approved, the project moves into a detailed design stage. The task here is to develop one or more levels of storyboard that prepare the way for the production and authoring of program material into CD-I digital data. Applications in Chapter 6 show the types of storyboard style that may be used depending upon the stage in the production process. The techniques described here are a typical way to carry this out. However, different design studios may carry out the same types of task in different styles.

The storyboard page in the French Phrasebook application would be used prior to the final authoring stage, when the precise nature of audio levels, screen coding requirements and interactive branching must be known.

Chapter 6: French Phrasebook

The example illustrated for the Hot Shot golf game uses a more generalized descriptive form to convey an overview of necessary information about screen layout, video planes, audio quality, synchronization and the possible transitions to subsequent sequences. These could change before they reach the final authoring stage.

Chapter 6: Hot SHot Sports

Storyboards would usually be developed alongside a flow diagram that lays out the branching patterns at each stage of a sequence. It is essential to know the pathways between stills or linear sequences, in order to estimate processor requirements, images and sound sequences that must be available for user choice, and the way in which users can escape from a section or get assistance if confusion arises.

Chapter 6: French Phrasebook

THE CD-I AUTHORING ENVIRONMENT

Before examining the detailed aspects of design itself, it is worth outlining the parts of the CD-I authoring environment that will become

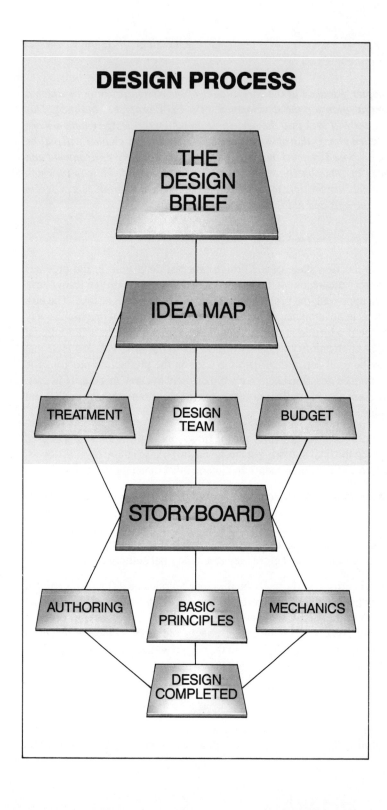

available to assist designers with the potentially complex tasks of working within data management threshholds for capacity and transfer rates. Some of these tools will be useful at the beginning of the design process. They will help the designer to simulate the general concepts of the program in rough form or as further briefing documents for graphic artists or live action directors. Other types of tool will be restricted to the final software authoring stages.

It is important to be aware that, at the time of writing, a variety of hardware and software design, production and testing touls are under development. A number of manufacturers and software houses have indicated delivery of protoype authoring systems and software during the second and third quarters of 1988. What follows is a description of the principles being follcwed rather than a precise specification of any particular hardware system or set of software tools.

Appendix C: CD-RTOS and Invision

The tools, collectively known as the authoring environment, will normally consist of a modular system, expandable from a single, low-cost workstation to a network of stations linked together into a complete production facility. It will be a distributed system, to allow teams of creative people to work simultaneously on an application, with easy access to common data and control information.

The authoring system will assist the designer in the writing of application code, the capturing of audio and video, and the editing or digitizing into CD-I formats, of these design elements. The edited data will be stored in the system's powerful database, combined with control elements into disc files. Testing, another function of the authoring system, will involve playing back assembled files on a simulator. It will consist of a read-write storage medium and special hardware which will emulate a CD-I player. The simulator will ensure that the application is tested in a real-time interactive setting.

The Designer's Station

The designer's station will commonly be a single, low cost workstation with CD-I simulation capability used by a design team for storyboarding, scripting, program development and testing. It can be used independently, by attaching a local disc and/or tape streamer to the station. Audio, video and other data will be transferred in digital format to and from the station via tape.

The Production Facility

The complete production facility will consist of several workstations and dedicated audio and video servers. The facility will also use a studio server, which will consist of a number of large read/write discs, write once optical discs for archival storage, and magnetic tape for output to the mastering plant.

Disc Building

The authoring system will be used for design, production and integration of an application through each stage of the disc building process. During the scripting phase, the designer needs to be sure that the elements of the application will not exceed the limitations of the CD-I player. For this purpose, an on-line Constraint Analyzer is being developed which can check the script against the known boundaries ofthe player. Disc band width, memory limitations, seek times and other key design considerations will be analysed using this software.

When design parameters have been set, the authoring system will guide the assembly process, which consists of data acquisition, presentation editing and disc building. Data acquisition involves the capturing, editing, and encoding of audio and video. Audio acquisition can be handled outside the CD-I authoring environment, as many studio facilities are capable of handling the complete digitization process.

Presentation editing links audio and video with programming. Simulation will be controlled by the presentation editing software, which will also provide data-specific editing tools, and tools for the building and testing of real-time records.

Lastly, disc building combines the control information with the encoded audio, video, text and application programming. These elements are structured hierarchically into records and files, and processed into forms needed by the master tape generator.

Standard Data Formats

The data used for CD-I applications will come from many sources. It will need to be translated into standard data formats to ensure compatability and quick, accurate data transfer. The standard formats include reading and writing routines and a standard library of access routines.

Scripting Subsystem

The term 'script' is defined here as a set of structure, display and control commands which are used by the programmer in creating CD-RTOS modules. Simulators will read the script as the CD-I control and command language. The scripting subsystem will allow the designer to describe the program structure, controls and logical flow.

Audio Subsystem

The audio subsystem will accept digital audio, and convert it to any of the allowable CD-I formats. This will be accomplished by the application of digital signal processing algorithms. Digital to analog conversion will occur by the connection of a D/A converter to the output stages of a digital audio processor. Non-real-time synthesized sound will be produced by generating PCM files within the authoring system.

Video Subsystem

Images acquired from standard video sources will be filtered and processed into digital images. Standard image processing techniques such as noise reduction and color balancing will be supported. Manual editing and enhancement of images will be accomplished using digital paint systems. Once an image has been digitized, filtered and edited, it will be encoded into one of the accepted CD-I image formats such as RGB, CLUT or DYUV. Previewing the processed images will occur using a CD-I simulator.

The Presentation Editor

The Presentation Editor will assist in the creation and integration of real-time records. It will also link data into blocks and display these blocks for testing purposes. Both functions will use a simulator and CD-RTOS modules to support communication between the simulator and host system.

The creation of real-time records is one of the most important aspects of CD-I development. A real-time record editor will be involved in synchronization techniques, interfacing with graphics routines, and the generation of correct file interleave factors.

The Database Subsystem

The central problem in the creation of CD-I discs is the management of the massive amount of data which a disc will contain. The amount and complexity of data can be overwhelming, as it combines scripts, storyboards, CD-RTOS modules and source files, as well as multiple versions and types of images and sounds. Copyrights for all of these would belong to different people and organizations.

The database manager will provide a central control and management facility for coherent access to CD-I data. It will parcel out the data to the various utility programs and provide data locking to prevent two programs from modifying the same piece of data. As modifications are made, the database system will maintain a history of such changes. Access to data will be controlled, to provide data security and privacy.

Testing and Simulator Subsystem

The simulator will provide quick turn-around testing of ideas during the creation process. It will also test the final disc image before mastering takes place. In the basic authoring environment, the simulator will be a 'compiled' facility. In the future, simulators may provide interpretive facilities. These would interpret database files to build the CD-I datastream, allowing faster interaction than the compilation technique, which requires each disc image to be rebuilt after every change.

BASIC PRINCIPLES

The authoring tools dealt with in the first section of this chapter will relieve the design team of some of the potentially burdensome calculations required to keep track of data in the CD-I system. Essentially, a designer wants to know what will happen on the screen or speakers of a television system and what will happen when a user participates in the various elements of interactive program material.

This is a major creative task. Software tools that can simulate the effects both at the general level and later at the specific authoring level, as well as provide feedback on data management, will release the design team to apply energy to solving creative problems rather than mathematical ones.

CD-I is not a form of video, like a VHS cassette player, but a computer-based technology: sound and pictures are simply aspects of a digital databank. That data can be transformed into video pictures, stereo sound, text, or it can remain in the digital domain to guide the direction of an interactive application.

The key to understanding CD-I and interactive design is to think about it as a computer process, rather than a television or print process. The design tasks can then be seen in terms of gathering and organizing different types of data that are made available to a CD-I user through the interactive computer interface.

While the CD-I designer need not immediately understand all the complexities of the technology, it is important to grasp the basic principles of CD-I design - the rate at which data can be transferred from the disc, the amount of data required for the various elements that make up a CD-I program, and the memory space available both on the disc and within the system. For example, how much space is required to store each type of data? How fast and to what locations can data be moved before decoding and playback? What proportion of the available memory locations and data channels are consumed by each type of CD-I effect? What will happen on the screen while data is being located at a new place on the disc? How many tasks can be handled by the main processor?

In this section some of the elementary calculations needed to keep track of storage capacity and processing power are introduced. Design for CD-I requires a regular monitoring of both of these by estimating the data amounts involved in creating desired effects. Eventually they will be handled by authoring stations. Nevertheless, a reasonable fluency with these numbers will give a greater depth of understanding about the types of effect that can be incorporated into CD-I progams. Appendix A gives a detailed account of the precise figures for storage quantities and data rates.

Basic Principles

• Tracks and Sectors

• Disc Capacity

• Data Transfer Channels

• System RAM

• Main Processor Power

Tracks and Sectors

In any CD-I disc, data is stored on a track of sequentially-recorded sectors. A sector contains approximately 2k bytes of data. The precise amount differs depending on whether it is Form 1 (usually audio and video program material) or Form 2 (usually text and program control data).

Chapter 7: CD-I Sectors

Chapter 7 deals with this subject in detail. What is important to remember here is that the CD-I player reads data at a constant rate of precisely 75 sectors/second, no matter where on the disc that data is located. This is equivalent to approximately 170k bytes per second (that is, 75 sectors multiplied by the precise sector size - which can vary slightly). So one sector (just over 2k bytes of program material) can be changed and interleaved in the stream of data coming off the disc at a rate of 75 times every second

A sequence of program sectors can be grouped together to produce a program module. The key to interactive program design is to break sequences into short modules that enable the user to couple them together through choices made at the screen interface.

Disc Capacity

The structure of the CD-I disc is explained in detail in Chapter 7, but essentially, the usable total storage space on a CD-I disc is 650 megabytes (Mb) of digital data - enough space for roughly 150,000 pages of text on a single disc.

Audio capacity is calculated according to the quality level used. One second of Level A stereo uses 85k bytes; Level B stereo 42.5k bytes; and Level C stereo 21.3k bytes. Mono at each level requires half these amounts. So if 650 Mb of disc space is available for sound, simple mathematical calculations can be made to determine how much of any particular audio level a CD-I disc may store.

Unfortunately, a megabyte is 1,048,576 bytes, not 1,000,000 bytes. Those not blessed with an understanding of computers must accept that there are 1024 bytes in a kilobyte and 1024 kilobytes in a megabyte (1024 x 1024 = 1,048,576).

So, to return to our task, if 650 Mb of disc space is available only for sound, then just over two hours' of Level A stereo can be stored (650 x 1024 = 665,600k bytes divided by 85 = 7830 seconds = 130 minutes = 2 hours 10 minutes), or a prodigious 17.5 hours of Level C mono, but of course with no other data to accompany it.

Single visual images occupy various amounts of disc space depending on how much of the screen each fills, the screen resolution (normal, high or double), and what coding technique has been used.

It should be remembered that an image covering only part of the screen requires only a percentage of the space of a full screen image. For example, a picture occupying half the width and half the height of the screen would take up 25% of the screen (not 50% as the mathematically unwary might suppose).

A single full screen DYUV image in normal resolution and occupying a full 8-bit plane fills 360 pixels x 240 pixels in NTSC (384 x 280 in PAL). Each pixel needs 1 byte, so the mathematical calculation is quite straightforward: 360 x 240 = 86,400 x 1 byte = 86,400 bytes per full screen natural DYUV image in NTSC (107,520 bytes in PAL). The 86,400 bytes (107,250 bytes in PAL) can be rendered into kilobytes by dividing by 1024. The answer is 84.38k bytes (104.74k bytes in PAL) - call it 85 and 105k bytes. So, in simplistic terms, if 650 Mb of disc space is available for natural DYUV images, at least 7,800 different full screen DYUV images can be stored on and replayed from a CD-I disc (650 Mb x 1024 = 665,600 kilobytes divided by 85 = 7,830). If only 25% of the screen is used, a CD-I disc can store over 30,000 separate DYUV images.

A single RGB image occupies both 8-bit planes and can be used in double resolution only. It therefore requires 170k bytes NTSC (210k bytes PAL) of storage space.

CLUT graphics occupy varying amounts of space depending upon the type and coding method. 8-bit and 7-bit CLUT, like DYUV, occupy full screen planes and require 85k bytes (105k bytes in PAL) of storage. 4-bit and 3-bit require only 1/2 byte per pixel or 42.5k bytes of disc space.

Using Run-length coding for 7-bit and 3-bit CLUT extends the capacity of a disc considerably. For example, a run of 10 pixels of one color - say, blue sky - would take only 2 bytes, one to indicate the color and one to note the length of run. The full economy becomes apparent in, say, a large expanse of a single color running for 50 lines at 360 pixels/line.

The maximum run of a single line is 255 pixels, however, setting the Run-length to 0 sets the distance to run to the end of the line. Each line would therefore need only 2 bytes of storage instead of the 180 bytes of a normally-coded 4-bit CLUT graphic. So 50 lines of one color would need 50 x 2 = 100 bytes instead of 50 x 180 = 9,000 bytes divided by 1024 = 9k bytes.

Of course, the actual requirement of any image depends on the data content of that particular image. With experience, it should be possible to estimate disc capacity fairly accurately. These concepts are explained more fully in Chapter 7.

Data Transfer Channels
The CD-I player reads one sector on the disc at a time and allocates it to a data transfer channel. There are up to 16 possible data channels available for audio information. Each other data type can have up to 32 channels.

Channels are a useful metaphor for the way in whichdifferent kinds of data must be interleaved into the data stream. For example, a television receiver may intercept all the available broadcast channels, although most TV sets can display only one at a time. In the same way, all the sectors in the data flow are picked up by the player and allocated to their respective channels, but only those called upon by the user during that particular run of the program will be used. (Although in CD-I, if not in most TV sets, more than one channel may be played at the same time.)

Language Learning

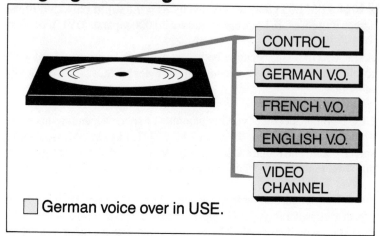

☐ German voice over in USE.

In the diagram, voice-overs in three languages are interwoven with background music and photographs. During the sequence, the user could decide to change from English commentary to German without interrupting the flow of music or pictures, since all three voice tracks are running in the data stream simultaneously.

Data Transfer Channels: Audio Playback

All audio in the CD-I standard is digitally encoded until it is finally played back through analog amplification and speaker systems. This results in there being negligible background noise at all quality levels.

CD-I Audio

Level Name (Requirement)	Sampling Rate	Bits per sample	Frequency Response	Number of Channels	Percentage of CD-I datastream used
CD Digital Audio 16B PCM (Super HiFi)	44.1 kHz	16	20 kHz	1 stereo	100%
CD-I ADPCM Audio-Level					
A (HiFi music mode) (Equivalent to LP)	37.8 kHz	8	17 kHz	2 stereo 4 mono	50% 25%
B (HiFi music mode) (Equivalent to FM broadcast)	37.8 kHz	4	17 kHz	4 stereo 8 mono	25% 12.5%
C (Quality speech mode) (Equivalent to AM broadcast)	18.9 kHz	4	8.5 kHz	8 stereo 16 mono	12.5% 6.25%

The critical factors in audio processing rates are the bandwidth (quality) that is reproduced at each level and the percentage of the data stream that is used.

A-level audio has a flat frequency response up to 17kHz (the limit of most discerning ears), while using only 50% of the data stream in stereo playback. C-level stereo, using only 12% of the data stream, is still able to reproduce excellent audio quality for most television applications. It is worth noting that B-level has the same wide frequency response as A-level but gains a slightly rougher quality by being stored in 4 bits instead of 8 bits.

Data Transfer Channels: Video Playback

Video data is transferred from the disc to the Image Stores before display on the screen. Video data must be mixed into the data stream with the audio and any software data that may be needed. The critical point to keep in mind for video processing is the time it takes to move a single image from the disc to RAM, given that it can only occupy that part of the data stream that is not used up by other data.

Chapter 7: CD-I Decoder: Video Processor

Both DYUV and 7- or 8-bit CLUT NTSC images require 85k bytes per full screen image. If no other data is passing through the channel at the time (i.e. no audio), it will take 0.5 seconds to load each image. This is calculated by dividing 85k bytes by the rate at which data can be transferred from the disc - 170k bytes per second. But if A-Level audio is playing, 50% of the data stream is already occupied, so it will take twice as long - approximately one second - to load each image.

Chapter 3: Motion Video

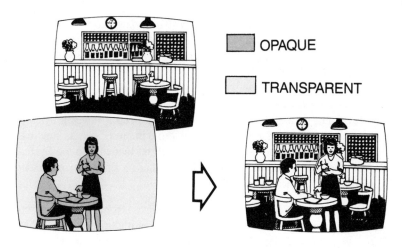

OPAQUE

TRANSPARENT

Creating motion requires the video screen to be refreshed around 15 times per second. Partial screen updates or run-length coding techniques reduce the amount of data required to store a single image in the motion sequences.

Each image can occupy only 170k bytes (the data rate) divided by 15 images/second, or about 11k bytes. Since a full screen DYUV and CLUT image requires 85k bytes in NTSC, then only about 13% of the screen can be occupied by moving images.

However, a series of software coding techniques have been developed that increases the amount of screen area available for partial updates from 13% to about 50% - and permits C-Level stereo sound to be played at the same time. These techniques effectively redistribute the coding parameters in such a way as to produce reasonable quality moving images instead of high quality stills. Using chroma key to confine the updates to the front plane can result in full-screen, full motion video with synchronized stereo sound.

System RAM

Chapter 7: CD-I
Decoder: Random Access
Memory

Aside from the permanent storage space on the compact disc itself, there is a temporary storage space within the CD-I system called System Random Access Memory (RAM), which offers a total memory space of 1024k bytes or 1 MB, divided into two banks of 512k bytes each. Data transferred to System RAM can be retrieved much more quickly than data which must be retrieved from the disc in real-time. As storage is temporary, everything transferred to System RAM is lost when the player is turned off.

Operating software in the CD-I system will use some part of the available System RAM space. While the main CD-RTOS operating system is contained in the system ROM, about 50K is loaded into system RAM when the player is turned on.

Application software requirements will vary according to the nature of the program, so a simple program may only need a few kilobytes of whereas a complex database retrieval program may use as much as several hundred. Some of this software will be loaded into the System RAM when the application begins, while other sections may be loaded and unloaded as the application progresses.

Chapter 6: Hot Shot
Sports: Audio

Most music and voice-over audio will be retrieved from the disc and sent directly to the Audio Processing Unit (APU), without using any RAM. However, some types of sound may be stored more accessibly as soundmaps in RAM for use at cued moments in the program or to await the user's actions: for example, a sound effect which signals a correct decision in a game. Effective use of soundmaps can help to mask the time taken for a disc seek.

Memory requirement for a soundmap is calculated on a percentage of the data rate. The memory needed for a sound effect which lasts for 3 seconds at C-Level stereo is calculated by taking 12% (C-Level Stereo) of the data rate (170k bytes x 12% = 20K bytes) and multiplying by three seconds - about 60k bytes altogether. Once this is transferred to RAM, it can be used as often as necessary in the course of the program without recourse to the disc.

Chapter 3: Audio: Soundmaps

Video is the most critical user of RAM storage data as all visual images must be loaded into RAM before being displayed on the screen. Each bank of 512k bytes supports one video screen plane.

Chapter 7: CD-I Decoder: Random Access Memory

Effects like dissolves or wipes require the second of the two pictures in the effect to be held in RAM and brought into play when needed. DYUV images use 90k (105k PAL) or about 20% of the available RAM space. When these images are loaded into RAM, their display timing is synchronized to the flow of the audio track, then they are unloaded to make room for new images.

Judicious design thinking is required to make efficient use of the limited RAM space available for both sound and pictures.

Main Processor Power

Video images can be synthesized or manipulated in the MPU before passing to the screen planes for display. Drawmaps are spaces in memory that can be manipulated by the MPU. In the golf game described earlier, the direction and size of the ball travelling down the fairway is determined by the conditions of swing and the timing of the hit that a player signals to the computer. A drawmap of the golfball held in RAM is manipulated by the MPU and a trajectory is calculated with data received from the user interface. Progressive variations in ball size and screen position are calculated and displayed as the ball appears to move down the fairway from the tee, rising in flight to meet the viewer's eye, then descending once again to land by the green in an excellent position for the second shot.

Chapter 6: Hot Shot Sports: Action Areas

The CD-I designer is faced with the task of creating applications for a consumer market whose expectations are based on broadcast television standards for sound and picture. The only real limitation to accomplishing that is the confined data flow, which hampers the use of unlimited full-screen full motion video. Managing the complicated data storage and processing power restrictions within CD-I will be dealt with in the next section.

THE MECHANICS OF CD-I DESIGN

One key to effective design for CD-I is controlling the display of information in sound and pictures by managing the storage and transfer of digital data in the CD-I system.

CD-I is an interactive medium: the design of audio and visual images must be directed to the activities of the person using the application. Interactivity is not yet common in home entertainment and home education, so designs must allow for the consumer's initial unfamiliarity - and, perhaps, nervousness - with the concept. People may not want to be constantly making choices, answering questions, looking for information or even playing games: they may want to watch a bit of television now and again.

These sorts of consideration should be allowed for in program design. The opportunity for a user to enjoy a variety of program styles will make successful programs. This section explains the various factors that must be brought together to present program material to the user.

Interface Devices

While the choice of interface devices of course varies widely across the range of potential applications and the degree of interactivity in any one, a basic device will have two buttons and a pointer to control a cursor on the screen. This might typically be a remote control pad, though other simple pointing devices might also be used. More complex devices might include a computer keyboard, a music synthesizer, a graphics tablet, and even special tools like light pens or bar-code readers.

Screen Design

It is inevitable that expectations for this medium will be based on broadcast television standards, not only for picture quality, but also for pacing and many visual and conceptual elements. CD-I applications hardly need be modelled after trend-setting TV shows, but some awareness of the conventions of that pervasive medium is important. CD-I does offer many screen effects that help to create the visual style of broadcast television.

Magazines and television advertisements are also good models for CD-I screen design: the screen can be regarded as an electronic magazine page on which elements of text, photos, graphics and even full motion video can be combined for a variety of effects. And while one of the limitations of CD-I is that full screens of information require large amounts of data, it is not always necessary to change the whole screen at one time: small areas of change will accelerate the pace of the presentation without straining the data flow capacity. Ultimately, pacing depends on the frequency rather than the volume of change.

Screen Effects

Screen effects - what the user sees - are the visual palette of the CD-I designer, and require management of the different types of image coding to be displayed on one or both of the two 8-bit image planes.

Chapter 3: Visual Effects

Image coding is explained in Chapter 3. What is important here is the relationship between images in dual plane configurations and the restrictions that govern which planes are used to display certain types of image.

Dual-plane DYUV

Chapter 3: Visual
Effects: Scrolling

DYUV images can be shown on both Plane A and Plane B, and these planes can be reversed while mixing images. However, problems of data rate arise in fast scrolling, and partial update effects (explained in Chapter 3) are difficult to achieve with natural images in CD-I. The subtlety of color coding in DYUV (and 8-bit CLUT) make it difficult for the system to calculate the necessary starting values, or their locations, for rapid updates to happen properly.

CLUT over DYUV

 OPAQUE   □ TRANSPARENT

In this configuration, the 8-bit 256-color CLUT is taken up entirely in the foreground or Plane A, leaving Plane B to be encoded in DYUV. As the Color Look-Up Table is completely used by the foreground image, no space is left for any other CLUT-coded graphics. As RGB images require a full 16 bits, a single DYUV image is the only possible image that could be displayed on Plane B. The CLUT/DYUV combination creates a high quality natural background, such as a landscape or interior room, with a flexible CLUT graphic in the foreground. In a language program, a graphic plate with a customer's bill could be shown over a DYUV image of a French cafe scene to show through. Plane A could be partially updated to show changes in the bill if the customer wished to dispute the total.

The only advantage in using 7-bit CLUT in the foreground would be to increase the animation speed of the graphic by Run-length coding.

This configuration would be used to present text information on Plane A in front of a DYUV image. Text or simple graphic icons in a children's entertainment program would benefit from double resolution without being affected by the reduction of color choice. 4-bit CLUT would also be useful for simple high-speed animation.

Dual 7-bit CLUT

This is a very flexible image configuration. CLUT graphics can be displayed on either screen. Scrolling is less limited with dual 7-bit CLUT, and restricted only by available memory space.

3- or 4-bit over 7-bit CLUT
This configuration is best suited to foreground text or simple foreground animations over a more subtle graphic background. Both 3- and 4-bit CLUTs have a narrow color range and are best suited to large areas of animation. Remember that 8-bit backgrounds cannot be used in combination with other CLUT planes.

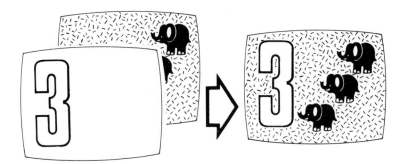

It is possible to use a 4-bit plane in the background if simplified colors are appropriate in both foreground and background - for example, for a text menu over a simple colored or fast-scrolling background page.

Dual DYUV with CLUT subscreen
In this combination, part of the screen appears as ordinary DYUV images, but another part is designated a sub-screen running the full width of the screen but only part of its height.

This sub-screen can be used for a complex graphic panel to control of the changing images on the remainder of the screen. For example, by using parts of the graphic toolkit, the detective in a mystery game could control the path of a surrogate 'walk' through a country house where the murder has been committed, interview suspects or gather clues.

Chapter 6: Country House Murders

Partial screens, requiring less data storage, save memory space in the graphic area and reduce the size of natural images to be updated in the DYUV part of the screen.

Controlling the Dataflow
The fundamental challenge for CD-I design is to bring together the design skills of existing media such as interactive video, television or book design, with the management problems of digital storage space and data flow particular to CD-I. To visualize the scope of possible applications, the CD-I designer needs to be at home with the calculations

which keep track of CD-I data. The design factors discussed here are applied to potential applications in the next chapter.

Interleaving

Information stored at the beginning of each sector tells the CD - Real-Time Operating System what that sector contains - the type of data (audio, video, text, software), whether that data is real-time, to what channel the sector belongs, and so forth.

CD-RTOS directs each sector in turn to its appropriate processing location within the player. It acts like a traffic controller, directing each vehicle in the linear stream to the correct lane in order to make the most efficient use of space available. However, the traffic is not random since the CD-I program designer has some control over the types and sequence of sectors in the CD-I traffic flow, and thus the efficiency of CD-RTOS.

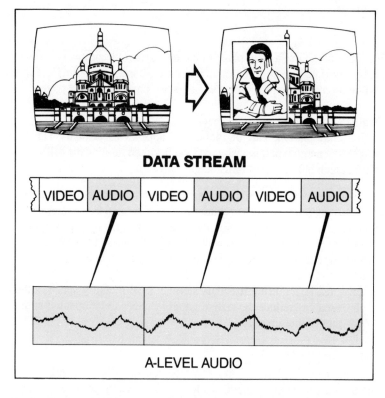

In the diagram above, A-Level stereo audio is to be played with a series of dissolving photographs of a neighborhood in Paris. Audio of this quality requires 50% of the data stream, but for the playback of the audio to be timed correctly, each audio sector must be followed by a single sector of other data such as the video data or possibly text or application software.

In this case, it is the audio that determines the speed of picture change, and the pictures are synchronized with the audio channel. Video requires approximately 37 sectors (50PAL) to load each DYUV image into RAM. Of the 75 sectors per second picked up by the player, half are already occupied with the audio - leaving only half (or 37 sectors/sec) for video. At that rate, pictures are available at intervals of 1 second. In an actual photo essay, it is reasonable to assume that pictures do not have to change more than once every three to five seconds. Furthermore, the full screen need not change every time. Thus, this combination of audio and video data is well within the capabilities of CD-I.

If this application were part of a large database like an encyclopedia, or a language phrasebook, then total storage space on the disc could affect the calculation: for example, C-Level stereo, rather than A-Level, would provide adequate sound quality and leave more disc space for other types of information.

Chapter 6: Grolier Multi-media Encyclopedia and French Phrasebook

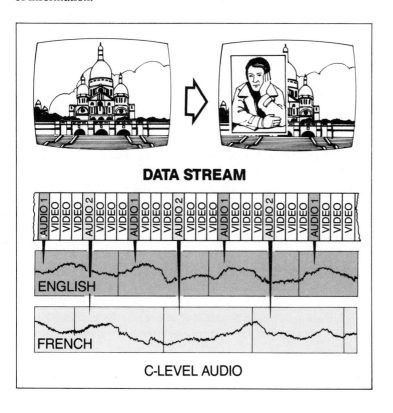

If C-Level stereo is used, only one out of every eight sectors in a sequence is required for the soundtrack. If pictures change by dissolving or cutting every four to six seconds, then other sectors in the data stream can be allocated to additional information that may be requested by the user, including completely different C-level mono sound.

Seek Time

The value of keeping a variety of programme choices grouped together in the data stream is the speed with which the CD-I player can respond to a user's request for change. If the data is not present in the data stream, the player must seek it in another part of the disc, which is likely to disrupt the programme.

Chapter 6: Pop
Showcase: Disguising
Disc Seeks

Seek time is the time needed for the pickup head of the CD-I player to move from one part of the disc to another, for the motor to adjust its speed accordingly, and for new data to be read and decoded in the system. CD-I discs revolve at variable rates depending upon the part of the disc that is being read - that is, they have a constant linear velocity (CLV), or constant data rate of 75 sectors per second. Moving towards the outside of the disc, the motor slows down; moving towards the inside, the motor speeds up. Picking up data stored within a 20 Megabyte (Mb) range (or within 3% of the disc) does not require the motor to change speeds significantly, so seek time is negligible. The total time to access new data may still be as much as one rotation of the disc (as much as 1/4 sec). At 170k bytes/sec, 20 Mb amounts to almost 2 minutes of real-time play or between 100 and 200 full screen DYUV images depending upon the quality of sound interleaved with the images.

Unlike interactive LaserVision, sound and picture can be stored in RAM and played through the system at the same time that the laser head is moving to another location on the disc to find the next sequence of material. Most seeks can be disguised in this way.

Synchronization

Various segments of CD-I program material travel along different paths and undergo different processes. Each type of data (video, audio, text, software) is broken down into units of about 2k and stored in sectors along the disc track. Thus, the playback of these sectors to the video and audio receivers must be synchronized to ensure that the audio track lines up with the right picture and that special effects in video or audio are correctly timed.

Within the data of any sector is a trigger bit, which tells the application software that this is a synchronization point and that something specific such as a special effect should happen here.

Synchronizing to Audio

In synchronizing with audio commentary, the video picture may change on a word or between specific phrases. The trigger tells the application software the exact time that the specific sector is being read by the player so the software can then cue the image change or any other effects that may be stored in RAM or generated in the MPU for that moment.

Synchronizing to Video

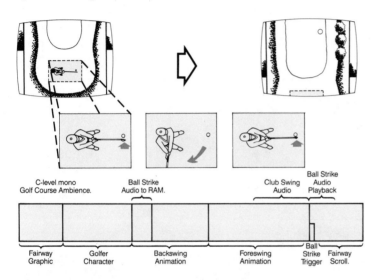

C-level mono Golf Course Ambience.

Ball Strike Audio to RAM.

Club Swing Audio

Ball Strike Audio Playback

Fairway Graphic

Golfer Character

Backswing Animation

Foreswing Animation

Ball Strike Trigger

Fairway Scroll.

The task is similar to that already practised in motion film or video. At the start of a sequence the audio must be correctly aligned with the video to ensure that a speech, for example, synchronizes with the lip movements of the speaker. Once the correct alignment has been made, sound and vision will proceed at a constant rate.

In CD-I, when the user may intervene to determine when a particular action takes place, the task becomes more complex. In a game like the golf simulation introduced earlier, the visual of a golf club swinging must synchronize with a carefully-timed audio effect as the club hits the ball. The timing of the synchronization cue depends on the instant that the player - acting through a remote control or other input device - designates as the exact moment the club head contacts the ball. This type of effect can be handled economically as a soundmap pre-stored in RAM and played through the audio output channels at the required moment.

Chapter 6: Hot Shot Sports: Audio

Timed Cues

The CD-I system has an internal clock which can be used to generate timed cues such as, for example, a limit on user response-time: if nothing

Chapter 7: CD-I Decoder: Clock/Calendar

happens within the designated period, the software proceeds to the next action on its own, perhaps advancing the programme, or perhaps shutting the system off.

Interactive Design

Interactivity covers a broad range of possibilities depending on the degree of user participation required. At one level, interactivity could keep the user guiding the program and responding to cues. The attention is active and highly engaged. Depending, of course, on the nature of the content, a linear sequence in an interactive application is usually best kept shorter than 20 or 30 seconds, before some kind of user action is required.

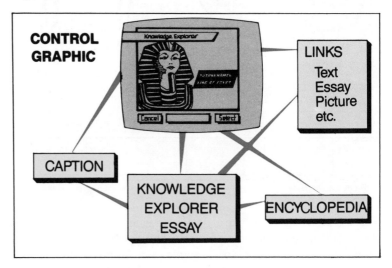

At another level, interactivity may require the user to select a picture essay on Science, Art or Geography from an encyclopedia. The essay might then play for 5 minutes unless interrupted by the user to branch into other essays, or into a more interactive search through text information.

CONCLUSION

This chapter has covered the basic technical principles of CD-I design. Along with Chapter 4, a comprehensive view has been given of the Design Process from the initiation of the Brief, through the Idea Map, to the development of various levels of Storyboard. Chapter 5 looked into particular technical constraints that are specific to design problems in CD-I. Using this as a groundwork, the next chapter will present several detailed examples of CD-I applications that illustrate various design and data management concepts.

CHAPTER 6: TYPICAL CD-I APPLICATIONS

The previous chapters outlined the nature of CD-I multi-media and the factors which contribute to good application design. This chapter looks at some specific design concepts and how individual applications discussed in other chapters illustrate these concepts.

It is difficult to find subjects which do not lend themselves to development as CD-I discs. What may be even more difficult to realize is that when existing products are converted to CD-I they become entirely new concepts, quite different from the printed work, audio-visual program or computer software on which they were based.

An encyclopedia, for example, is no longer a series of articles, long and short, in alphabetical order, with pictures to illustrate a few. It may begin with a choice frame offering several voyages of exploration through picture, sound and text databases. You can study any topic you choose in a variety of ways - gaining a general overview in a short audio-visual essay, perhaps, before going on to see what more specific information is available, and choosing an area to study. You can pick a word - your own surname, for instance - and see how many times and where it is mentioned in the text database. You can even select information such as a picture, text and audio commentary, to create a short presentation of your own.

Similarly, the experience of watching a classic film, play, dance work or opera, for example, can be greatly enhanced through CD-I. The disc might contain, as well as the performance itself, critical essays about the work, short notes on key passages (which you can call to the screen at the appropriate time), interviews with key personalities, biographies of the principal performers and production team, and background information about the making of this production. You may listen to the original script or libretto, and call up sub-titles in the language of your choice. You can even dub out the stars and take over yourself, and make your screen debut opposite Garbo, Olivier or Callas!

The following are just some of the topics that lend themselves to CD-I. They certainly show the range and diversity of the CD-I publishing opportunity.

- pop music, movies, plays, dance and opera, enhanced as described above

- studies of famous people and events in history and popular culture

- art and music programs which allow the user creative control

- games of observation/deduction, such as mysteries and adventures

- educational games for children, to teach learning and social skills as well as academic subjects and knowledge areas

- interactive movies and even erotica which allow the user or player to direct the action

- games of skill such as bridge or chess, or enhanced versions of board games such as Monopoly

- multi-media reference works such as encyclopedia and dictionaries

- diagnostic reference books on specialist topics from family medicine to car repair

- picture libraries and databases for amateur and professional collectors, scholars and hobbyists

- games of general knowledge, wit and experience, such as trivia and word games

- armchair travel guides and tourist books

- guides to famous places and buildings, from archaeological sites to museums

- maps, plans and navigation aids - including in-car systems

- 'surrogate travel' through fabulous places (real or imaginary)

- arcade-style games demanding hand/eye co-ordination and quick judgement

- educational material at all levels from pre-school to post-graduate

- language teaching for self-tuition or institutional use

- industrial and commercial training material, both off-the-shelf and made-to-order

- catalogs and sales aids, for use by customers and in co-ordinated sales presentations, and for staff training

And these are only a few ... A videotape has been developed which simulates some of these applications, keeping entirely within the 'Green Book' specification. Chapters 4 and 5 developed a notion of the Design Process through three main stages - The Brief, The Ideamap, and The Storyboard. The following example applications illustrate various aspects of CD-I design issues presented earlier. The encyclopedia deals with the major issue of total storage capacity for one project on a single disc. The Hot Shot Golf game will show an example of an early stage storyboard, where ideas are sketched out for such design considerations as screen style, program sequencing and possible interactive branching routes. The French phrasebook will show an example of a later, more specified stage in the storyboard process when the overall design is complete and ready to be released to production.

THE GROLIER MULTI-MEDIA ENCYCLOPEDIA

The world's largest publisher of encyclopedias, Grolier, has already identified CD-I as the logical choice for a multi-media edition of their Academic American Encyclopedia. Grolier is currently designing the world's first interactive encyclopedia on CD-I because CD-I provides an immense capacity for the storage of text, pictures and sound and because CD-I allows the user to browse interactively. Even when stretched to the maximum search time, the CD-I encyclopedia will call up information much more quickly (and of course more accurately) than a reader can with the 20-volume original print version. Furthermore, CD-I can illustrate the text database with sounds and pictures, audio-visual experiences that add an entirely new dimension to information retrieval. The Multi-media Encyclopedia will tempt passive viewers to explore deeper layers of information through interactivity.

Designing the Interactivity
The key question in designing an encyclopedia is to be very clear about how the interactivity will work. Rapid and accurate text retrieval is an early priority, but many people love just to browse, and to have their curiosity stimulated by what they come across. Yet there must also be opportunities to take a break from the interactivity and be entertained. Audio-visual essays have been designed to provide hours of entertainment by taking the viewer on journeys around the vast amounts of knowledge by combining the text, pictures and sounds into short presentations.

Mode of Use
The text, picture and sound databases provide a natural foundation for the development of an overall structure for the various types of information to be contained on the disc. This will lead naturally into development of the first level of interactive branching to retrieve information from each of the areas.

With the Multi-media Encyclopedia, information will be divided into several inter-connecting databases ('Domains of Knowledge') in a web that enables the user to move freely among them. These databases include:

- A series of audio-visual essays on general topics within main categories such as, for example, Arts, History, Geography, Science, Sports and Ideas;

- An audio database of speeches, sound effects, music and song;

- Picture captions and links leading into databanks of maps, pictures, graphics, games and a 'Time Machine' feature;

- The full encyclopedia text itself - over 10,000,000 words fully indexed.

Data Management
The critical data management issues for an encyclopedia concern absolute disc capacity rather than dataflow rates. However powerful CD-I may be, and however large its storage capacity, the megabytes still get used up awfully quickly when you are trying to cram an overview of the whole of human experience onto a 12cm disc!

Screen Interface
To allow entry to these various Domains, two types of screen interface are essential. One enables direct access to any of the Domains from the moment the disc is loaded. The other allows access from within one Domain to any of the others - a lateral structure. Each must be compatible with a simple input device like a mouse or tracker ball.

Menus

Menus provide instant access to any of the Domains so, for example, the user can pursue a specific topic or question. If the user simply wants to browse, the Knowledge Explorer offers a choice of short introductory essays on general topics. The menu here cycles a series of still images from each of the essays in the appropriate box, which act as visual stimuli to suggest what each essay contains.

Choosing just one of the essays begins a sequence of passive television viewing that can continue as long as the user wishes. The interactive aspect is up to the user to choose, otherwise the encyclopedia offers linear video without requiring constant or even intermittent attention.

Screen Effects

The short essays use the screen effects within the CD-I player to show photographic DYUV natural images and CLUT graphics.

Dissolves, wipes and screen montages give a television style to the presentation; however, as these effects are generated within the CD-I player itself, the individual images remain untouched, and can appear in a variety of forms - in the essays, or within any number of picture bank on various subjects.

This application could contain several thousand separate images, each of which could be used in several ways.

Graphic Control Panel

After simple access menus, the second type of screen interface is a flexible control panel which allows various degrees of interactivity.

If, for example, the user stops one of the 'Knowledge Explorer' essays at any point, the image on the screen freezes and the 'control panel' appears as a graphic and matte over the picture.

The control panel is coded as a 7-bit CLUT displayed on Plane A. Since the panel can be called up at random, the software must ensure that the image from the audio-visual essay is moved to the background if it is not already there.

Interactive Branches

Several areas of the control panel are 'active regions' and correspond to directions that the user may explore.

Touching the option 'Caption' brings up a caption in the transparent area of the foreground panel. This contains additional information about the picture or subject on the screen. Each caption is interleaved with the data for its associated picture.

In the same way, the 'Links' button brings up a list of options for connecting to other parts of the encyclopedia. This list is also interleaved with its associated picture.

Although the pictures in the essay change slowly, and use C-level stereo for background audio and voice-over, the data stream is also occupied with other data elements which may not be used every time but which must be available to the user.

Domain Seeks

To reach some of the Domains offered by the Link option, or to research in the text Domain, the player pickup would have to move to another area of the disc, using a delayed seek time. This is acceptable as a major change is being made.

The CD-I Multi-media Encyclopedia is able to hold a vast amount of information on one disc: up to 10 million words, 3000 pictures, and three hours of sound - enough for a complete 20 volume printed encyclopedia with audio-visual essays and interactivity as well. However, the large volume of data being stored, and the complexity of access, requires careful management and design.

HOT SHOT SPORTS

The treatment for Hot Shot Golf has already been described in Chapters 2 and 3. Athletics is another topic that lends itself well to inclusion in the CD-I range of applications. The Olympic Games give pleasure to millions of television viewers around the world, but imagine how their pleasure can be enhanced even further with the CD-I Athletics database.

In the early stages of the High Jump competition, you can park the television picture carrying a live transmission from Seoul and call up the High Jump database. Who is the record holder ? What happened last time there was a jump off for gold in the Olympics ? Study the form of the contestants. Use the 'Slo Mo' feature to step frame by frame though motion pictures of the last finals. Call up 'Chalk Talk' and have the CD-I coach talk you through technique. So when the time comes for the jump off, your pleasure is greatly increased by the insight and understanding you have gained from Hot Shot High Jumps.

Back to golf. This application makes use of interactive computer animation as well as high quality photographs and ambient background sound. What is significant about this version of the game is that the graphics of the computer arcade game are combined with photos of a real course to allow the viewer to play alongside the professional. In fact, the storage capacity of the disc is sufficient to offer the player a choice of famous courses as well, from Augusta to St Andrews. The animation program for the game would use the same factors no matter which course was selected.

The accompanying outline storyboard shows the earliest stages of idea mapping, with sketches of a key image for each sequence of the game. These indicate the main types of plane configurations, sound quality, and the transition type (that is, whether the scene is part of a linear sequence or a pivotal frame allowing branching to other parts of the application).

The production tasks then fall into two areas. The first is to accumulate a database of photographs covering a representative sample of possible positions from which shots could be taken as a player moves through eighteen holes. The second is to develop an interactive game animation.

Photographic Database

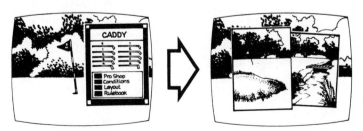

Each game needs about 750 photographs, shot specifically for this project. For each of the eighteen holes, there is a tee shot plus five separate views spanning the fairway at 100 yard intervals, and a good

CDI PROJECT TITLE: *Hot Shot Sport*   Sheet: **9.4**

1

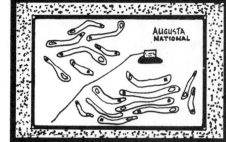

Sequence: Main Choice Frame
Plane A: CLUT - 7 - Matte
Plane B: CLUT - 7 - text scroll

Source: Commission Graphic

Time on screen: User Choice - max. hold 60 sec
Audio: S/map - theme 5 sec / off 60 sec
              C - stereo
FX:
Transition: Branch - Sport menu - Cursor On

2

Sequence: Matchplay Choice frame
Plane A: CLUT · 8 - matte
Plane B: DYUV - still - 25%

Source: Library Photo / Commission Graphic

Time on screen: User Choice - max 30 sec
Audio: Off

FX:
Transition: Branch - Course Intro

3

Sequence: Course Module 1 : Augusta
Plane A: CLUT - 8 - 100% map
Plane B: Off

Source: Commission Graphic

Time on screen: User Choice - max 60 sec.
Audio: C - mono

FX:
Transition: Branch   - Hole Caddy
                        - Course History
                        - Return to Choices

4

Sequence: Hole Module - 15
Plane A: CLUT - 7 - menu 20%
Plane B: DYUV - 15th tee - 100%

Source: Commission Graphic / Library Photo

Time on screen: User Choice - max hold 30
Audio: C - mono ambience

FX: birds
Transition: Branch   - Game
                        - Pro Shop
                        - Course History

CDI PROJECT TITLE: **Hot Shot Sport**   Sheet: **9.5**

1

Sequence:	Pro Shop - 15th Hole
Plane A:	DYUV - 15th tee - 100%
Plane B:	DYUV - sandtrap - 50% key
Source:	Commission Photo
Time on screen:	5 sec / image
Audio:	C - stereo
	V.O. - Commentary
FX:	ambience
Transition:	Linear dissolve / return to Hole Mod.

2

Sequence:	Course History
Plane A:	DYUV - Nicklaus - 75% + 25%
Plane B:	CLUT - 7 Factfile text
Source:	Library Photo / Comm. Graphic
Time on screen:	5 sec / image
Audio:	C - stereo
	V.O. + music
FX:	crowd cheer
Transition:	Linear dissolve / return Hole mod.

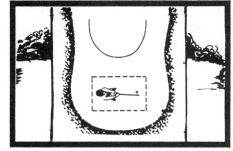

3

Sequence:	Game - Animation
Plane A:	CLUT - 3 Golfer
Plane B:	CLUT - 7 - 15th Hole / vertical scroll graphic
Source:	MPU software / Commission graphic
Time on screen:	Interactive - max hold 30 sec
Audio:	C - mono ambience
FX:	swing / hit / crowd
Transition:	Branch return / linear to next position - DYUV

Golfer Animation

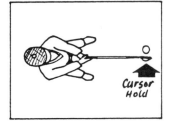

Start Backswing

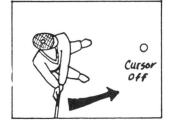

Start Foreswing

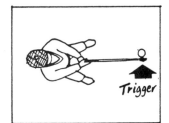

Ball Contact

selection of photographs on and around the green. Each photograph should give the player a good view of the next shot from the point at which the last shot ended.

These photographs can also be used in an informative way: the caddy menu, for instance, besides dispensing the chosen club, also offers advice from the club professional on the best way to play that particular hole. Short documentary sequences could relate anecdotes about famous golfers or famous tournaments at the course.

Screen layouts consist mainly of DYUV images of the course on the background planes with graphics of menus or the animated figure of a golfer on the foreground.

The Animated Figure

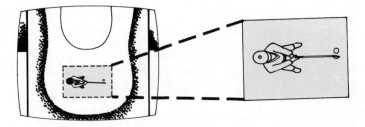

The golfer is an interactive animated figure which is handled by the microprocessor within the CD-I player (and remains the same no matter what course is represented in the photographs). The figure is seen from above (unlike the figure in the popular computer golf game) to allow the computer to spend its power on interaction with the user rather than on a complex graphic. With Hot Shot Golf, the player actually determines the flight of the ball by controlling the swing.

The golfer is a 3-bit CLUT animation in the foreground. In the background, the DYUV image looking down the fairway is changed to a 7-bit CLUT and replaced in the centre with a 7-bit graphic depicting an aerial view of the hole which will scroll vertically when the ball is struck.

Changing the DYUV view to CLUT keeps the background plane in the same coding system and CLUT scroll alleviates some of the difficulty of DYUV scrolling.

Action Areas

Two 'action areas' have been determined for the golfer. The first is the hat: placing the cursor on the hat and holding the button down on the remote control device allows the player to align the golfer's feet and thus the direction of the ball, taking into account factors of wind direction.

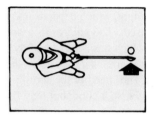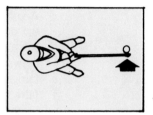

The second action area is the ball: when the cursor is moved to the ball and the button held down, the golfer's backswing is activated; when the button is released the foreswing begins; at the moment the player sees contact between the lub and the ball, the thumb button is tapped once again.

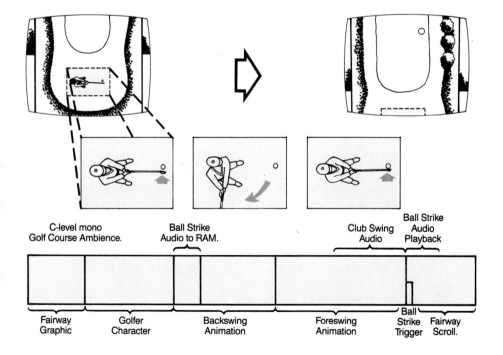

This is a point of critical timing, both for the player and the designer. The microprocessor has to deal with several calculation factors. One is direction, based on alignment of the golfer's feet and by the point of impact: touching the button too early causes it to slice to the right, touching too late hooks it to the left, and correct timing sends it down the middle.

Another calculation is speed and distance of flight, which depends upon the amount of backswing and the club used. The microprocessor calculates these factors and displays a ball, which has been stored as a drawmap in RAM, increasing and decreasing in size as it flies down the fairway, coming to rest before the next shot. The speed of the scrolling fairway is co-ordinated with the speed of flight, so a poor shot may fly off the fairway to one side.

Audio

As audio is not critical for quality, C-level mono is used for a background of birdsong and the like. However, sounds such as the swing of the club through the air and the impact on the ball make the moment of contact more vivid. Four sound effects are loaded as soundmaps at the beginning of the swing: the loop of the foreswing cutting the air, the sound of the club hitting the ball, and a choice of crowd sounds appropriate to the quality of the shot - either a round of applause or a murmur of disappointment!

Of course, this type of interactive animation against a realistic background could be developed for virtually any single-player sport and, with some imagination, for team sports as well, with the user taking the role of a key player or even the coach.

COUNTRY HOUSE MURDERS

The murder mystery is a classic game, well suited to CD-I. The combination of interactivity and multi-media allows the designer no end of opportunities to thrill and suprise the audience. In the version designed for the demonstration tape, one or more players act as detectives trying to solve a murder in a stately country house; the computer randomly selects details of the crime, which change with every playing.

Surrogate Travel

The atmosphere of the house is created through a technique known as 'surrogate travel'. The house has ten main rooms plus corridors, cupboards and staircases. As the camera travels through the house, a series of photographs is taken, at eye level, and at carefully graduated intervals, to simulate the impression a real visitor would have wandering through the house and in and out of its many nooks and crannies. These DYUV images will 'cut' in sequence on the background plane as the detective moves about the house. There is no jumping from room to room here: many things can happen to unwary detectives in the poorly lit corridors of old houses!

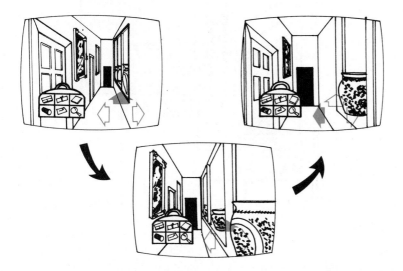

Movement is controlled by a CLUT direction graphic on the foreground plane. Touching the arrows allows the player to turn left or right or to walk forward.

Handling Disc Space

Storing photographs on the disc is a problem of disc geography. Images are sequenced so that the cuts can happen quickly and smoothly. Turns may require a short seek to the start of a new series of images. It would be preferable to jump at this point rather than after the turn and the start of the new 'forward' sequence.

Possible false turns, where no further forward motion is possible, could be interleaved into the series: for example, the detective could stop in a corridor to look at a painting which might contain clues... or fall down the cellar staircase by taking too sudden a turn.

Icons

Routes through the house and the task of clue gathering is helped by various graphic icons in the detective's 'tool kit'. At the start of each game, the detective is offered a choice of potentially-useful objects to put into the kit - of course, there is not room for them all. For example, a plan of the house (which can be overlaid on any frame to show the player's present location) would be useful- and so would a flashlight.

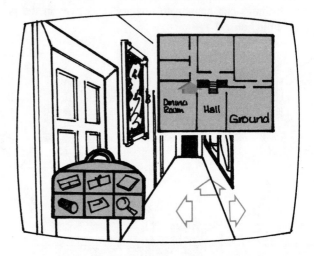

Other tools might include a cassette tape-recorder for interviewing witnesses and suspects, a fingerprint kit, a notebook and even clues gathered during the course of the investigation. As with many adventure games, the detective may not be able to carry everything at once, and may have to decide what to foresake, and where to leave it.

Audio

Audio quality is not critical in this game, but could be used for interviews, or random special effects like squeaking hinges and floorboards, or distant cries of distress, to add flavour to the hunt. The game might offer different levels of interactivity with, say, special sound effects to draw attention to important clues or even hints for the youngest or slowest players!

POP SHOWCASE

This application is about pop music, so the sound quality is a critical design issue. Pop Showcase is designed in two parts: the first concentrates on the music of a particular band or performer, the choice of A-Level stereo for optimum listening quality; the second is an information bank with details of the stars' background, greatest hits, tours, gossip and so forth.

Since A-Level sound uses fully 50% of the data stream, the design of the accompanying screen displays is critical, particularly as the screen must seem to move frequently in keeping with the general tempo of the music.

Partial Screen Updates

A magazine style was chosen both to suit the lively tone of the program and to meet the practical need to keep the update areas small. As a particular song plays, DYUV images change in different areas of the screen as a pictorial collage to accompany the music, and also as a menu or table of contents for other material contained on the disc.

Disguising Disc Seeks

Highlighting any one of the images on the menu will stop the song and lead the listener into various related information areas, which might include a biography of one of the band members, or a scrolling list of hit records.

The music is used as background sound so the audio quality can be reduced to C-Level here as the graphic and DYUV components of the screen demand a larger portion of the data stream - and the viewer's attention.

Moving from the Menu to specific information requires disc seeks. To keep the audio playback alive, the pickup head plays bursts of sound as it skips to a new area of the track. This is a way of disguising seek time - by making it audible!

Singalong

A feature of Pop Showcase is a singalong section: as a song plays, the lyrics are displayed line by line with a bouncing ball that keeps time to the music.

The magazine format of the screen is maintained here, and greater interest is added by incorporating segments of CD videos coded in CD-I digital form onto the background plane. As the listener is probably singing, and not listening too closely, audio quality is again reduced to C-Level stereo,which leaves maximum room for the DYUV full-motion video and CLUT graphics in the stream.

However, as full-motion video is intended here, some careful calculations must be made to determine how the effect is presented to the viewer and what proportion of the screen can be occupied.

Screen Proportion

The foreground plane is a 7-bit CLUT graphic. It holds the scrolling texture plane with a matte through which a mixed DYUV and CLUT background in the other plane is visible.

The second plane through the matte is then divided into two subscreens: an upper part in DYUV containing part of the still pictures and the motion video, and the lower part in CLUT together with the rest of the still, the bouncing ball and the text. As the part of the still that is in the DYUV subscreen was CLUT coded originally, the joint between the two parts of the image is not visible.

The bouncing ball is created from a computer program within the CLUT subscreen.

The computer program for the bouncing ball and the scrolling of the front plane are pre-loaded into the program space in System RAM. The text bars are pre-loaded as drawmaps. While running the sequence, the partial update motion video and the sound are read directly from the disc, and synchronized to the program.

The partial update used here is 70% of the data stream. Thus 70% of 170k bytes/sec. yields 119k bytes per sec., which at 15 frames a sec. represents 8k (9.5k PAL) bytes/screen area/frame. In terms of screen area this is 8k (9.5k PAL) divided by 90k bytes (105k PAL), or about 9% of the full screen. This would be a rectangle just under 1/3rd by 1/3rd of the total screen.

The sound, C level stereo, takes 12% of the data stream. This is slightly under the full data rate, as the processor is heavily occupied with ball animation and the scrolling effects in this example.

As the video is not critical to the singalong sequence, this size of image would be very attractive in collage page format.

INTERACTIVE UNDER FIVES

Pattern, word and number recognition are learning concepts that all children under five years of age work hard to acquire. CD-I offers a unique and potentially highly effective means of providing attractive learning games.

One-to-one relationships with parents and teachers remain important features of learning at this age, but CD-I can provide hours of exciting supplementary practice. Bright graphic animations using 3-bit CLUT coding would enliven the acquisition of reading and counting skills no end.

Shape Recognition

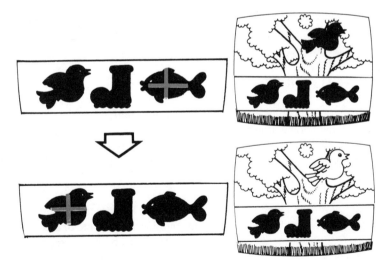

In this sequence, a yellow bird is sitting in a tree created as a 7-bit CLUT in the background. A 3-bit CLUT sub-screen stretches across the bottom holding three silhouettes of familiar animals, one of which is the same as the bird sitting in the tree. An oversized cursor moves across a sub-screen at the bottom of the other plane. The object is to match the images.

The simplified cursor has been designed as very young children have difficulty co-ordinating a pointer in the usual way: thus, the cursor is incorporated into the graphics as a drawmap icon which moves about the screen in fixed or random patterns. When the icon is in the appropriate area of the screen, the child simply hits the specially designed large green control button.

The cursor shape is loaded into RAM. The microprocessor calculates the speed of the moving image and its position and displays the drawmap in that position on the screen, updating the image as it moves across. Certain areas of the screen can be activated so that, if the cursor is in that area and the button is touched, the system is cued to carry out the next action.

Sound is not critical in this sequence, so a background tune in C-Level mono is adequate, but for added interest, three sound effects are loaded into soundmaps in RAM as the scene begins - one of them is happy bird song. A voice-over acts as a guide to each game.

Each icon is active when the cursor appears in its silhouette area. If the button is touched while the cursor is in the bird silhouette, the bird will begin to flap its wings and sing its cheerful song.

As audio can be kept to C-Level, and the images are mainly animated graphics, CD-I storage and data rates are not strained - and nor is the production budget.

FRENCH PHRASEBOOK

CD-I offers a very flexible system for language tuition in the relaxed atmosphere of home or in an educational context such as a school. It has the capacity for simultaneous multiple language versions, live action dialogue scenes, and of course the interactivity that allows the student to practice in real-time simulations.

The CD-I French Lesson is patterned on standard home teaching systems which use books and audio cassettes to combine the pleasure of learning about a foreign culture with useful phrases for an upcoming business trip or holiday.

This particular phrasebook contains:

• typical conversations in cafes, streets, stations and the like;

• special phases for familiar situations such as asking for directions or changing money;

- the opportunity to learn new words simply by touching specific objects in a scene;

- accumulation of useful phrases as they are learned in a scrolling notebook;

- a database of maps, museum guides and other tourist information;

- documentary essays about places of interest.

A single phrasebook can be marketed in several countries since the use of C-Level mono audio allows simultaneous coding of voice-overs in four or five languages. Corresponding text screens can easily be provided as well.

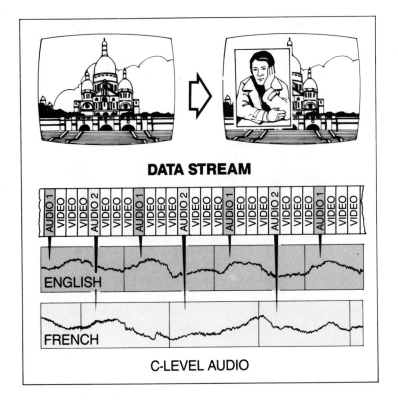

A five-minute picture essay on Montmartre begins with voice-over in French, but if the tired student feels that enough vocabulary has been learned already, this can easily be switched to another, more familiar language without interrupting the flow of the visual sequence.

Chroma-key Facility

Students learn new words and phrases through scenes which dramatize typical conversations, which they can control through interactive menus and some computer control programs.

Scenes are acted out in full-motion video - and in a screen area of the order of two-thirds by two-thirds. This is accomplished by using an additional software decoding method and CD-I's chroma key facility: the actors are shot against a single color background which can be keyed over a still DYUV background in the C-I player.

Real-time Dramatizations

The waitress approaches the customer, who asks what he can have to drink. The student is presented with a screen menu of drink choices in the form of an 8-bit CLUT high quality graphic which wipes onto the screen, replacing the closeup of the waitress on the front plane. The student can choose a drink.

Routes through the options available to the student are controlled by computer program code which directs the branching of the operating system to the appropriate start locations of each dialog sequence. Each set of responses is coded onto the disc, one after the other, and each lasts three or four seconds.

There are 3 possible sequences on the drinks menu:

- First sequence - the waitress asks: 'What would you like?'
  - ○ A menu of six choices appears and the student chooses café au lait
  - ○ First branch - first choice: the system moves to the beginning of the sequence for café au lait:
    Customer: 'I would like a café au lait.'
    Waitress: 'A café au lait, very well;
  - ○ The waitress confirms the customer's request and the whole menu reappears.

(Her response is useful both to the learning exercise and to shift the angle of view back onto her. After the student's next interaction, the customer can reappear at a new angle and appear to exchange remarks with the waitress. Changing the angle of view this way avoids jarring cuts to a new version of the same scene.)

- Second sequence - with the second menu in view, the student can re-consider and selects jus d'orange.
  - ○ Second branch section - all choices made after the first one: the system moves to the start of the jus d'orange sequence:
    Customer: 'No, I think I would like an orange juice after all.'
    Waitress: 'Ah, you would prefer an orange juice?'
- Third sequence - this time the student confirms by re-choosing the orange juice:
    Customer: 'Yes, please.'
    Waitress: 'Very good, I'll get it for you.'

Of course, the student could work through all six choices on the menu without exhausting the patience of the long-suffering waitress.

TITLE: *Bienvenue à Paris*   Sheet: *8.17*

~~PAL~~/NTSC   Normal/~~High~~/Double   Producer: *Lewin*

Section: *Dialogues*   Sequence: *Cafe - Drinks*

cursor	off	on ✓	

PLANE A

Visual: *Motion Video*

Update: *15/sec*

% screen: ~~10%~~ ~~22%~~ *36%*

Customer + Waitress

CLUT 8	
CLUT 7	
CLUT 4	
CLUT 3	
RL 7	
RL 3	
DYUV	✓

Source: *Chroma Key - Studio*

backdrop	off	on	

PLANE B

Visual: *Still Photograph*

Update: *Hold*

% screen: *100 %*

Cafe background ①

RGB	
CLUT 7	
CLUT 4	
CLUT 3	
RL 7	
RL 3	
DYUV	✓

Source: *Commission*

TRANSITION	linear/branching

TIME ON SCREEN: *5 sec/module*

TRANSITION EFFECT: *Linear Update*

2. Interrupt to freeze

_____ *Linear Next frame*
_____ *Main Icon Bar*
_____ *Cafe menu*
_____ *Cafe Icon Bar*

AUDIO	level: *C*	mono/~~stereo~~

SCRIPT   *Drinks - Lip Synch.*

W: Bonjour, Monsieur, vous desirez
C: Qu'est-ce que vous avez comme boissons

FX _____

Cafe ambience - S/map

CD-I PROJECT TITLE   *BIENVENUE À PARIS*   SHEET: *8.18*

SECTION: *DIALOGUES*   **SEQUENCE:** *CAFE / DRINKS*

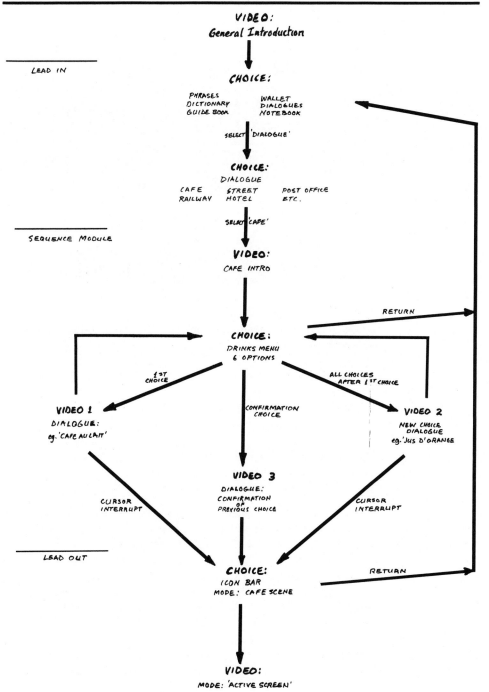

VIDEO:
General Introduction

LEAD IN

CHOICE:

PHRASES   WALLET
DICTIONARY   DIALOGUES
GUIDE BOOK   NOTEBOOK

SELECT 'DIALOGUE'

CHOICE:
DIALOGUE

CAFE   STREET   POST OFFICE
RAILWAY   HOTEL   ETC.

SELECT 'CAFE'

SEQUENCE MODULE

VIDEO:
CAFE INTRO

RETURN

CHOICE:
DRINKS MENU
6 OPTIONS

1ST   ALL CHOICES
CHOICE   AFTER 1ST CHOICE

CONFIRMATION
CHOICE

VIDEO 1
DIALOGUE:
eg. 'CAFE AU LAIT'

VIDEO 2
NEW CHOICE
DIALOGUE
eg. 'JUS D'ORANGE'

VIDEO 3
DIALOGUE:
CONFIRMATION
OF
PREVIOUS CHOICE

CURSOR   CURSOR
INTERRUPT   INTERRUPT

LEAD OUT

CHOICE:
ICON BAR
MODE: CAFE SCENE

RETURN

VIDEO:
MODE: 'ACTIVE SCREEN'

These optional routes can all be laid out on the disc in reasonable proximity to each other. Each section contains about six double phrases in the exchanges between the customer and the waitress, each requiring three or four seconds of real-time decoding.

Basic programming technique can identify a choice from one of the action areas on the menu, then seek the first sector of the appropriate sequence.

The customer could also ask for the bill, the option at the bottom of the menu, which would initiate a graphic and voice-over. (The wrong bill might be presented, which the customer could dispute by highlighting the amount where it appears on the screen.)

The customer can pay the bill through the 'wallet' menu on the icon bar at the bottom of the screen, by pointing to a note of a given denomination, which calls up an appropriate audio response:

- From several denominations, the customer selects one, saying: 'Here are .. francs'. Each possible phrase is so short that all the possibilities can be loaded into RAM for instant response time.

The icon bar (a 3-bit CLUT graphic sub-screen) provides access to the many different modes of operation in the lesson - a dictionary which activates areas of the screen to provide an illustrated vocabulary, a guidebook to Paris, even a scrolling notebook to copy the last set of phrases for easy reference.

The attached flowchart and storyboard page show how part of this sequence might be laid out. The storyboard page lists most of the key factors in the design of this module such as plane configuration and percentage of screen occupied. Transitions are indicated at the bottom showing the next positions that the progam could move to depending upon the user's choices. This takes into account both linear and interactive branching sequences.

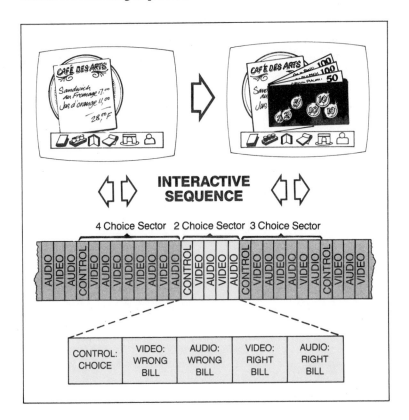

The flowchart page is a module sketch diagram used to plot the possible actions. It forms the basis of a briefing document for the software author. The precise routing of choices for the phrasebook application may change several times before the final version is tested and proved successful.

CONCLUSION

This chapter has described a range of applications as a way of further informing the reader of specific design concepts. In these early days of CD-I, applications will tend to be based on familiar resources - material from other media which can be converted to CD-I, or projects modelled on established formats from publishing, broadcast television or AV and computer software.

CD-I is powerful because it is a multi-media publishing vehicle. All the media can be integrated and everything is in the digital domain. CD-I is the first medium to combine the impact of video with the power of the computer in the same language of digital code. This demands new ways of thinking about information storage and retrieval. This powerful new medium will change our lives and the way in which we do things.

CHAPTER 7: HOW CD-I WORKS

For those readers wishing to understand more of the technical aspects of CD-I after having read Chapter 5, this chapter describes the CD-I Specification, or Green Book, in more detail. The subject is approached from the computer-orientated aspect of the technology.

A description of the disc structure and organization is provided, including file structure, the design of a typical CD-I decoder and a brief description of the Compact Disc Real-Time Operating System, CD-RTOS. Further information on CD-RTOS is given in Appendix B.

DISC STRUCTURE

The organization of a CD-I disc is designed to be compatible with existing CD-Digital Audio (CD-DA) discs and players. CD-I is based on the highly successful CD-DA specification and is a complete system specification, which includes the encoding process, disc content, and the CD-I player. CD-ROM, in contrast, only specifies a division of the disc into sectors. The encoding and decoding methods are not defined, and are to the individual applications developers to establish.

Disc Organization

The CD-I disc can contain some 650 Mb of data in any combination of audio, video and computer information. All compact discs - CD-I, CD-DA, CD-V and CD-ROM - contain a lead-in area, a program area and a lead-out area. The program area of a CD-I or CD-DA disc can hold up to 99 tracks, numbered from 1 to 99, and while a CD-I disc can include CD-DA tracks, the first track must always be a CD-I track. Any CD-DA tracks on the same disc must appear after the CD-I tracks. Typically a CD-I disc will contain one CD-I track plus, optionally, one or more CD-DA tracks. Each track can be of any length between 4 seconds and the total available program space.

CD data (as opposed to music information) can be recorded in two modes: Mode 1 - which is used in CD-ROM - contains extra error detection and correction codes, and is suitable for data which are highly sensitive to errors (such as computer databases). Mode 2 is suitable for information such as audio and video data, which is not so sensitive to errors; however, the the CD-I specification has defined two specific Forms within Mode 2, Form 1 and Form 2. Form 1 also contains extra protection for sensitive data. All CD-I data are recorded in Mode 2.

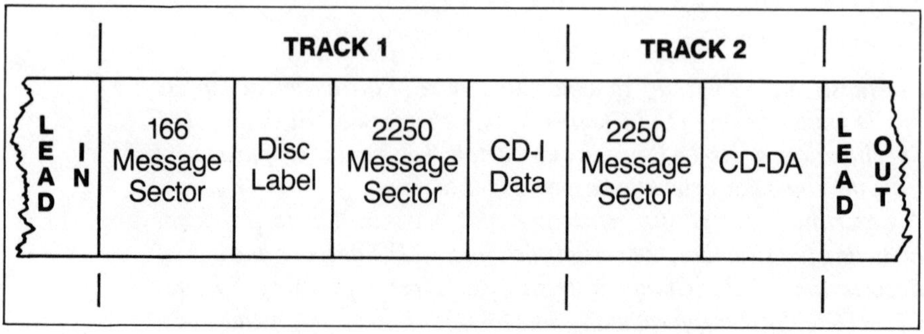

	TRACK 1				TRACK 2			
L E A D I N	166 Message Sector	Disc Label	2250 Message Sector	CD-I Data	2250 Message Sector	CD-DA	L E A D	O U T

The track organization - which is mandatory for all CD-I discs - is indicated in the figure. The beginning of the program area (that is, the start of track number one), opens with 166 message sectors which contain CD-DA information only.

The disc label (described later), comes next, followed by 2250 message sectors (or 30 seconds), after which comes the CD-I data. Between the end of the CD-I data and any CD-DA tracks, there must be a further 2250 or more message sectors.

Message sectors are intended to protect existing CD-DA players when they play CD-I discs containing data which might otherwise harm the CD-DA player or associated audio system.

Disc Label
The disc label is recorded in Mode 2, Form 1 - that is, with extra error protection - and contains a description of all the files on the disc, its contents, size, creator and so forth, as well as the location of any software modules which must be loaded into the system, and the path table which allows access to those files.

The disc label must, of course, be in Track 1 at the position shown in the diagram above.

The disc label comprises three records: the File Structure Volume Descriptor, the Boot Record and the Terminator Record.

Path Table and Directories

Relative Position	Parent Directory Number	Directory File Name
1	1	Root
2	1	CMDS
3	1	Games
4	1	Library
5	3	Checkers
6	3	Chess
7	3	Globono
8	4	Frank
9	4	Gibson
10	9	Text
11	9	Video

A path table must be recorded on each disc. This provides an index of the Directory Structure on disc typically following the disc label. Its location on disc is given by the disc label. This is illustrated by the example shown in the figures. The path table comprises a list of all the directories.

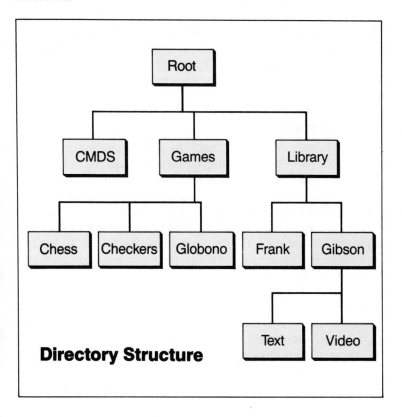

Directory Structure

Each entry includes the following fields:

- Location of Directory File
- Parent Directory Name
- Directory Name

Each Directory is a file containing file descriptor records.

Files

All data on a CD-I disc are divided into files. Any file may be accessed through the path table recorded on the disc. Each file is represented by a File Descriptor Record contained in the appropriate Directory file which contains the file name, number, size, address, owner, attributes, interleave and the access permissions for read. Files may, in fact, be interleaved on the disc so that it is not necessary for one file to end before the new file begins.

There are several types of file: directory files, real-time files and standard files.

CD-I SECTORS

CD-I data are divided into discrete units called sectors. These sectors are similar (but not identical) to those specified for CD-ROM. In the case of CD-I, these sectors contain as well as either audio, video or computer data, the vital information which the system needs to handle this data efficiently in real-time. (One CD-I sector is equivalent to one frame of CD-DA.) CD-I data are recorded and transmitted at a rate of 75 sectors per second.

CD-I Sector Format

Each CD-I sector has a total length of 2352 bytes, and apart from synchronization information, also contains a header and sub-header, followed by data. The header provides information on the sector address in minutes, seconds and sectors relative, to the start of the track. It also indicates the Mode - which in the case of CD-I, is always 2. The sub-header comprises the following: the data type (that is, audio, video or program-related data), the form (which may be 1 or 2), trigger bits (including end of record and end of file) and the coding information (the format of which depends on the data type).

Form 1 sectors contain 2048 bytes of user data and an additional 280 bytes of error detection and correction code, and are intended for data whose integrity is essential, such as application programs, other control data and text, where there is no built in redundancy to allow for errors.

Form 2 sectors contain fully 2324 bytes of user data, but no extra error correction, and so are more suitable for less sensitive data such as audio and video. Where the presence of errors will not seriously affect the operation of the player, Form 2 sectors still allow errors to be detected so allowing error concealment techniques to be used.

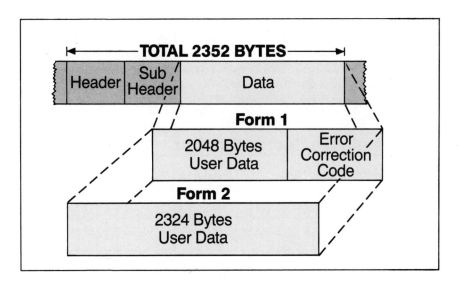

For example for video data a line or pixel in error may be replaced by the adjacent line or pixel.

CD-I Audio Sectors

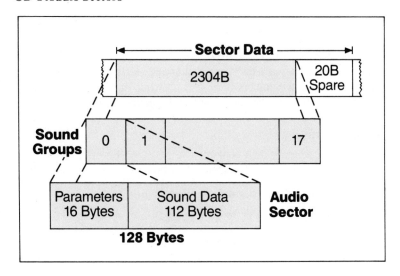

In CD-I, audio data is held in Form 2 real-time sectors. The sub-header contains information on the emphasis, the number of bits per sample (that is, either 4 bits for levels B and C, or 8 bits for level A) and the sampling rate (which is either 37.8 kHz for Levels A and B, or 18.9 kHz for Level C). Finally, the coding information indicates whether the sector contains mono or stereo sound.

The data in each sector comprises 2304 bytes plus a spare 20 bytes, and is divided into 18 sound groups of 128 bytes each. Each sound group is further subdivided into 16 bytes representing the sound parameters and 112 bytes of actual sound data. The audio data include range and filter parameters, which are optimized in the encoding process for each sound group.

Relative Sector Number

Level		0	1	2	3	4	5	6	7	8	9	10	11	12	13	14	15	16
Level A	S	X	O	X	O	X	O	X	O	X	O	X	O	X	O	X	O	X
	M	X	O	O	O	X	O	O	O	X	O	O	O	X	O	O	O	X
Level B	S	X	O	O	O	X	O	O	O	X	O	O	O	X	O	O	O	X
	M	X	O	O	O	O	O	O	O	X	O	O	O	O	O	O	O	X
Level C	S	X	O	O	O	O	O	O	O	X	O	O	O	O	O	O	O	X
	M	X	O	O	O	O	O	O	O	O	O	O	O	O	O	O	O	X

◼ **Audio Sector**

The audio sectors are interleaved as shown in the figure. For real-time audio, Level A stereo sectors are in alternate sector numbers (that is, in the relative sector numbers 0, 2, 4, 6 ...) while at the other end of the range, Level C mono sectors are encoded only in every sixteenth sector.

CD-I Video Sectors

CD-I Video data are also contained in real-time Form 2 sectors. The coding information for video sectors comprises:

- the resolution (that is normal, double or high);

- the coding method (DYUV, CLUT, etc.);

- an even/odd lines flag, which is used for error concealment.

The video data is transferred directly to memory and decoded in the video processor. Visual images are coded on disc as described below.

DYUV Images

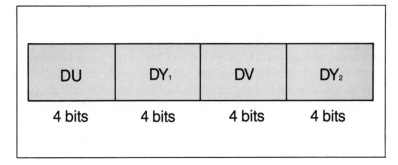

Each pixel pair is represented by 2 bytes (16 bits) organized as shown in the diagram. DY, DU, DV are the differential (or delta) values of luminance and color difference. Each 4-bit value is converted to an 8-bit value (representing 0 to 255) which is added to the previous value in the decoder. In calculating these delta values, the encoding process must take into account quantization errors to avoid the effect of cumulative errors. Also, since negative values are achieved by 'wrap around', the encoder must avoid a pixel pair.

CLUT Images

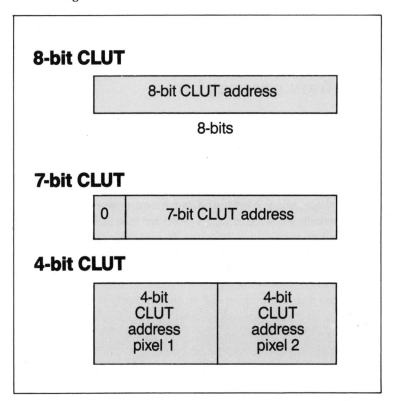

There are a number of different CLUT modes. CLUT-8 uses 8 bits of information to define the full pallette of 256 colors.

CLUT-7 or 7-bit CLUT provides 128 colors, also at normal resolution. For double resolution, CLUT-4 or 4-bit CLUT provides only 16 colors but allows twice as many pixels horizontally as normal resolution, which can be valuable for text screens particularly in complex character sets such as Japanese where details become more visible in double resolution.

CLUT images are coded with 1 byte per pixel (normal resolution) or 1 byte per pixel pair (double resolution) as shown in the diagram.

RGB 5:5:5 Images

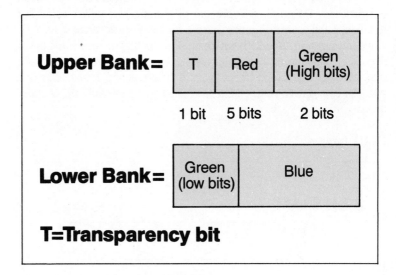

The two banks are coded separately.

Run-Length Images

In normal resolution, 2 bytes of data are used to define first the color (taken from the pre-selected CLUT table) and then the number of pixels which will appear in that color before the next color change - that is, the number of pixels for which the color will be retained. In double resolution, pixel pairs are defined together.

Run-length images are coded as 7-bit (normal) or 3-bit (double).

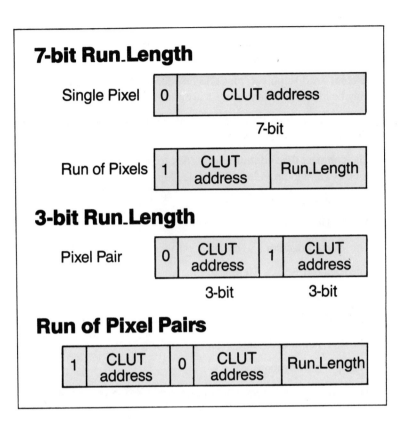

Program-Related Data Sectors

Program-related data sectors are always Form 1, since they need a higher level of protection than simple audio and video data. Computer data in CD-I may comprise application programs, control data, text or character fonts, in real-time or non-real-time, depending on the application.

Real-time sectors generally contain control data and synchronization information which is associated with audio and/or video sectors.

CD-I DECODER

CD-I decoders must be designed so that all discs can be played on all decoders. This implies that each decoder must be designed to meet one specification and certain parts of the decoder will be common to all.

The CD-I specification defines a base case decoder - that is, the minimum configuration which can be called a CD-I decoder. The figure contains a block diagram of such a decoder. It comprises:

- A compact disc player, plus CD-DA decoder and controller. (These may be identical to those found in current CD-players.)
- The audio processor, including ADPCM decoder and audio processing unit and attenuators.
- The compact disc control unit needed to provide the random access for CD-I and to provide real-time decoding of the sector information.
- The microprocessor.
- The DMA controller.
- The video processor and access controller.
- The Random Access Memory
- Non volatile RAM.
- The clock and calendar.
- The X-Y pointing device.
- The optional keyboard.
- The Read Only memory containing the CD-RTOS operating system.
- System Bus

These are described on the following page.

A number of extensions are possible to the base case decoder, including high resolution video and peripherals such as printers and modems.

CD-Drive/Player

The CD drive allows access to any part of the CD-I disc within at most three seconds. Drive control functions include pause, continue, stop and eject. The CD-DA decoder and controller decodes the CD-DA data, providing 16-bit PCM (Pulse Code Modulation) with left and right channels to the audio processing unit. It also provides all the necessary error correction facilities for CD-DA and low level correction facilities for CD-I sectors, and the low level control of the CD-drive.

The CD-control unit provides selection of the required channels (that is, channels 1 to 16 for audio, and 1 to 32 for video). It provides de-interleaving of the audio-visual programmable data streams and selection of file number and selective interrupt generation. The use of

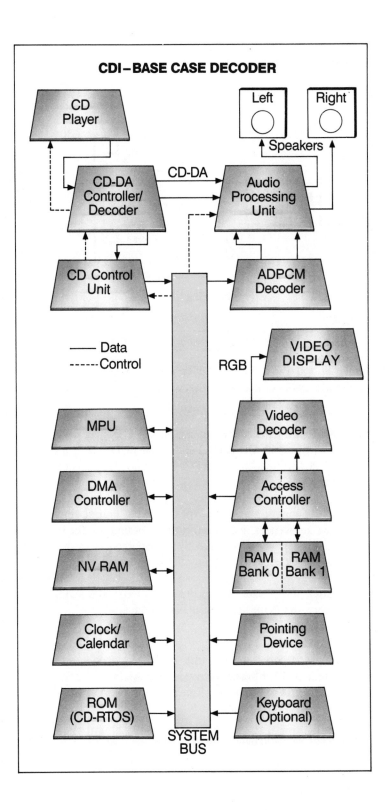

CDI – BASE CASE DECODER

the sub-header in each sector is very important to select the data type and to de-interleave the audio, video and program related data.

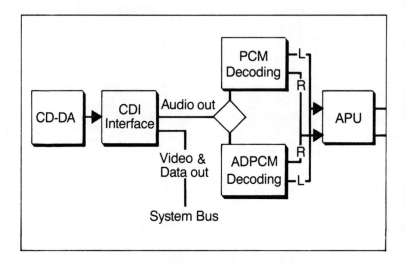

It should be noted that the CD-player with the CD-DA decoder and controller is capable of playing a normal CD-DA disc as well as CD-I discs.

The CD-DA controller decoder outputs CD-DA PCM data to the audio processing unit, and the CD-control unit outputs CD-I data, which can be either ADPCM, (Adaptive Delta PCM) audio, video data or program related data.

The CD-control unit recognizes the type of sector which is being read by decoding the sub-header and manages it accordingly - for example, ADPCM audio data may be sent directly to the audio processor or to the memory, while video and program-related data will be sent to the memory.
The de-interleaving of data ensures that the video, audio and program related data are sent to the appropriate parts of memory.

Audio Processor

The audio processor comprises the ADPCM decoder and audio processing unit. ADPCM data is passed to the ADPCM decoder either directly from the CD-control unit or from memory. The ADPCM decoder decodes Level A, B or C audio.

This outputs PCM audio data, both left and right channels.

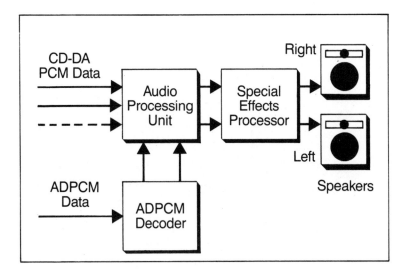

The Audio Processing Unit

All audio passes through the Audio Processing Unit (APU) on its way to the playback system. The APU acts like a simple two-channel audio mixer within the CD-I system, with two input channels, either stereo or mono, from two sources, and can mix the input channels to the left and right output channels in any one of four ways.

In addition, the APU can vary the loudness of each channel separately, for mixing and speaker panning effects. Individual units of sound, stored on disc, can be used in various ways for specific application software. Without the APU function, all audio combinations for a specific application must be pre-authored and stored on the disc in case it is called up by the user. A great deal of redundant storage space is saved this way.

Video Processor

The video processor includes the access controller and video decoder. The access controller provides an interface between the main system bus, the memory and the video decoder. The random access memory is divided into two banks: Bank 0 and Bank 1. Bank 0 contains information for Plane A, and Bank 1 for Plane B. The memory is also used for storing soundmaps and for system memory.

The video decoder provides all the facilities for decoding the various pictures and special visual effects described in Chapter 3. The schematic diagram of the video decoder is shown in the figure. It comprises two real-time decoders, each capable of decoding visual images coded as described elsewhere in this chapter.

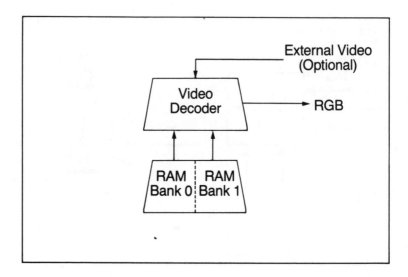

Real-time decoder 0 decodes DYUV, CLUT and Run-length images and real-time decoder 1 decodes DYUV, CLUT, Run-length and RGB images. RGB images, of course, require the use of both memory banks and provide only one full screen image per plane.

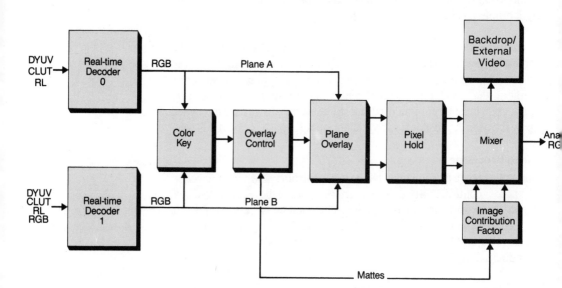

The output from each decoder is 8 bits each of Red, Green and Blue. For DYUV, CLUT and Run-length the output of each real-time decoder is at least 6 bits per R, G and B. RGB 5:5:5 provides only the most significant 5 bits of each component. The three least significant bits are always zero. The two planes A and B may be overlayed in either order (i.e. A in front of B or B in front of A) and means are provided such as the color keying and mattes for creating transparent areas in each plane. Alternatively, the planes may be mixed and the brightness of each plane defined by multiplying by an image contribution factor which allows for, e.g. fading. The pixel hold function is provided between the overlay and the mixer as shown. (Pixel repeat for CLUT and RGB 5:5:5 is provided within each of their decoders.)

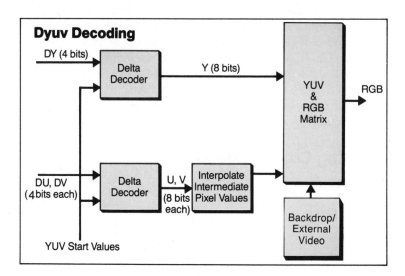

The backdrop and cursor are added at the last stage where the digital signals are also converted to analog Red, Green and Blue. For the base case decoder, the analog signals must have at least 64 levels (equivalent to 6 bits of digital information). Optionally, the decoder may provide the full 8 bits at 256 levels for each R, G and B.

The real-time decoder for DYUV is shown in the figure. The basic coding unit for DYUV is a pixel pair requiring two successive bytes in memory. For each pixel pair there are two values for Delta Y, one value for Delta U and one value for Delta V. In the decoder, for each of the Y, U and V signals, the delta codes are converted to their non linear quantization values; that is values between 0 and 255 (see figure) and the successive delta values are summed to give the absolute Y, U and V values. For each line, if not black, the absolute start values for Y, U and V must be provided and coded separately on the disc. U and V are linearly interpolated to fill in the intermediate pixels, because only every other pixel is sampled. Finally, Y, U and V are matrixed to RGB for displaying.

For RGB 5:5:5, each pixel is represented by 16 bits; 5 bits for each of the R, G and B components and one bit to provide transparency. This requires the use of both banks of memory to provide only a single image plane. RGB 5:5:5 decoding is, therefore, very trivial.

For CLUT coding, we have 1 byte representing 1 pixel for CLUT 7 and CLUT 8, and 1 byte representing 2 double resolution pixels for CLUT 3 and CLUT 4. CLUT 7 is available in both image planes, whereas CLUT 8 is only available for plane A.

Chapter 3: Run-length Coding

For Run-length images, Run-length 7 uses the 7 bit CLUT and a run is represented by 2 bytes; the first byte giving the CLUT address and the second byte giving the length of the run which can be up to 255 pixels long. For CLUT 3 (which allows double resolution) the first byte provides the colors for a pixel pair and the second byte gives the Run-length. For both 7 and 3 bit Run-length coding, all lines end with a zero length run, which means that the color should be continued to the end of the line.

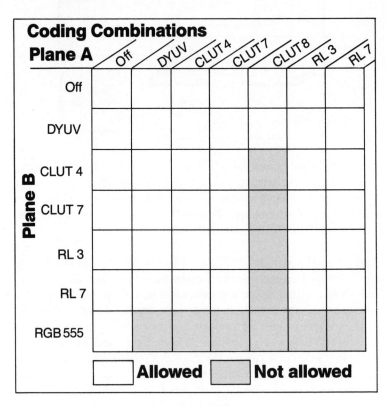

To use CLUT coding, whether directly or Run-length coded, it is necessary to know which entries in the CLUT are actually used. There is one color look up table in the decoder which has 256 entries, so for 8 bit coding the whole of this CLUT is allocated to plane A. (Note: It is not possible to use the CLUT for both planes A and B since this would mean time sharing it. Speed constraints prohibit this.) For 7 bit coding the CLUT is divided into two halves, giving 128 entries for plane A and 128 for plane B. Therefore, it is possible to have simultaneous 7 bit CLUT images. 4 bit CLUT coding uses the last 16 entries in each half and Run-length 3 uses the last 8 entries in each half. An application program can load appropriate color values into each entry of the CLUT, as appropriate.

The figure indicates the allowable combinations of the different coding methods. There are only two real restrictions on combining images. The first is that a CLUT 8 image cannot be combined with any other CLUT image or Run-length, as it uses the whole CLUT (all 256 entries). It therefore can only be used with DYUV in plane B or, of course, with plane B off. The second restriction is that RGB 5:5:5 uses the data stream from both image memories, so it cannot be overlaid with any other digital video plane.

RGB levels

As mentioned before, the output from each real-time decoder is an RGB signal converted into analog with a color resolution of at least 6 bits per R, G and B component. This means that each component can have a value from 0 to 255. The CCIR have recommended, for TV studio operation involving digital signals, that black level should be represented by 16 on a scale from 0 to 255 and peak white by 235.

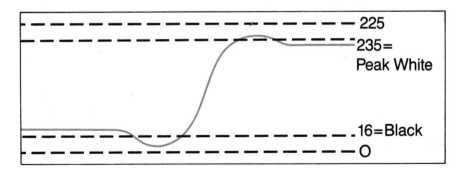

This allows some space below 16 and above 235 for inevitable undershoot and overshoot which is caused by bandwidth limitations of the TV signal chain. (For example, a square wave signal would overshoot both white and black levels when the bandwidth is limited.)

To avoid distorting images, the CD-I specification follows these CCIR recommendations. These are indicated in the figure. These levels are particularly important for natural images encoded with DYUV but to maintain consistency, they are used for all image coding methods. The RGB levels must be taken into consideration in the encoding of visual images.

Display Control Program (DCP)

The control of visual images include the loading of CLUT values, the defining of mattes, etc. The CD-I specification defines what is known as the display control program, or DCP. This consists of a set of display control instructions which are carried out on every field scan of the display. These instructions are placed in two tables which are the field control table, which is executed once every field, and the line control table, which has separate instructions for each line of the display.

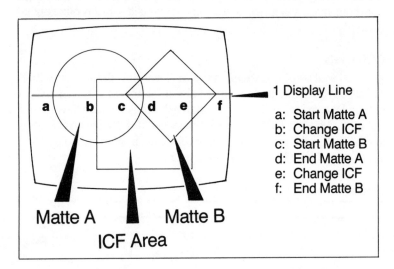

1 Display Line

a: Start Matte A
b: Change ICF
c: Start Matte B
d: End Matte A
e: Change ICF
f: End Matte B

Matte A   Matte B
ICF Area

There is a field control table and line control table for each of two image planes. The field control table can hold up to 1024 instructions and is used for setting up the display parameters at the start of each field and can include the data for loading into the color look up table for example. The line control table comprises up to 8 instructions for each line. These allow the display parameters to be changed from one line to the next as the scan progresses.

One of the most basic uses of the line control table is to provide a display start address for the beginning of the image line. It is possible, therefore, for the start of each line of an image to be in random locations in memory. This is particularly important for providing scrolling of images, particularly together with the use of subscreens, where only part of the screen is scrolling, where there will be a discontinuity between the fixed part and the scrolling part of the screen.

One important application of the DCP is the creation of mattes. An example is shown in the diagram. Here the display comprises two overlapping mattes and what is known as an ICF (image contribution factor) area. If we look at one line of the display marked in the figure, there are six points on this line where there is a boundary of one of these areas. Matte **A** is circular, matte **B** is a diamond and so on, but each of these mattes or areas, can in fact, be almost any shape. Along this display line point a indicates the start of matte **A**; **b** is the start of the ICF area, at which point, the ICF is changed to a new value. At point **c** is the start of matte **B**; **d** the end of matte **A**; **e** the end of the ICF area and therefore a change back to the old value of ICF and **f** marks the end of matte **B**.

Scanline Position 1
(Rabbit held in position)

Scanline Position 2
(Rabbit free to move)

Signal when this line reached, to
avoid flicker when redrawing.

Matte **A** and matte **B** could, for example, represent areas of transparency/translucency, revealing the plane beneath and can be used to generate some of the visual effects which were described in Chapter 3. Since the positions **a**, **b**, **c**, etc. can be changed from line to line, there can be a large number of mattes on one picture. The limitations are that only two mattes at most can overlap and there can be, at most, 8 matte boundaries on any one display line. The figure, of course, indicates six such boundaries.

Since each line of the LCT comprises up to eight instructions, it would be possible to change all of these boundary values on each line. However, this would leave no room for other instructions which may be required, for example, to set a new line start position.

Another example of a DCP instruction is shown in the diagram. This provides synchronization to display scanning. In the figure the example shown is an object being moved to a new position, for example, to produce animation.

To avoid flicker in the signal it is important that the object should not be moved while the object itself is being scanned. Therefore, it is possible on any line to insert an instruction which will generate a signal when that line has been reached. Therefore, the application can wait for the signal and can then move the object to the new position ready for the next scanning field.

Further examples of DCP instructions are as follows: the image coding method can be changed at any point on the display. This is how subscreens are produced.

A new backdrop color can be loaded. CLUT colors can be changed as the scan progresses to extend the number of colors available in any one image. A CLUT image plane can also be changed from 256 to over 2000 colors.

The Hardware Cursor

The small hardware cursor plane, 16 pixels square, was described in Chapter 3. Each pixel can be set to be either transparent or the cursor color which may be defined from a range of 16 colors. The cursor may be appear solid on the screen, or may blink, and it can be in normal, double or (as an extension) high resolution.

The position of the cursor can be set to any position within the full screen area of the display.

Border Color

The border around the reduced screen area can be set differently for each line and for each plane; however, if DYUV coding is used, this border must be black.

DMA Controller

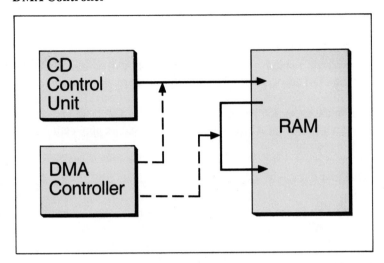

The DMA controller allows fast, efficient transfer of data within the system, between the CD control unit and memory, and from one part of memory to another, without the use of the MPU, thus releasing the MPU for more important work. Its function is shown in the figure.

Random Access Memory (RAM)

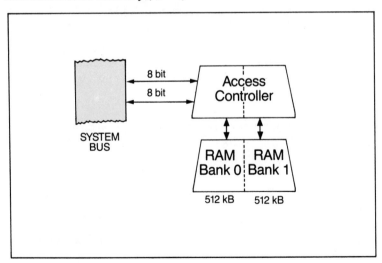

The random access memory (RAM) comprises two banks of 512k bytes each. It is accessed through the access controller using the micro-processor unit and the video processor. Each bank comprises 256k words, 16 bits wide. Image data has to be stored in the appropriate bank

(Plane A or Plane B); other data, such as soundmaps and system data, may be stored in either bank.

Non-volatile RAM (NV-RAM)

A non-volatile random access memory (NV-RAM) is also included within the CD-I decoder. It comprises a minimum of 8K memory, either non-volatile or backed up by a small battery to provide continuous support in the event of a power failure. Part of the NV-RAM is reserved for system information. The remainder may be used for application data. Data is organized as files in the NV-RAM.

Clock/Calendar

A battery-operated clock calendar, accurate to at least one minute in a month, records hours, minutes, seconds, the month, year and leap year.

Pointing Device

One or more X/Y pointing devices are provided as user interface for each CD-I decoder. Each will also include two trigger buttons and must be capable of pointing at any pixel on the full screen display at normal resolution.

The pointing device may be a mouse, joystick, lightpen, tracker-ball or any other suitable device, giving either absolute or (in the case of a mouse) incremental position, or velocity of movement.

Transfer Paths

At this stage it is worth a review of the material covered in this chapter up to this point by looking at the various pathways that data can follow within the CD-I system.

Data moves through the CD-I system from storage on disc or in RAM, from synthesis in the Microprocessing Unit (MPU), or from screen actions by the user. Application software tells CD-RTOS when and where to find data and which pathway to send it along.

Application Software

Application software is taken from the disc when the program begins and loaded into RAM to direct the program. Software can be loaded in and out of RAM during the course of the program depending on variable routes chosen by the user. This data is mixed with the audio and video data in the data stream.

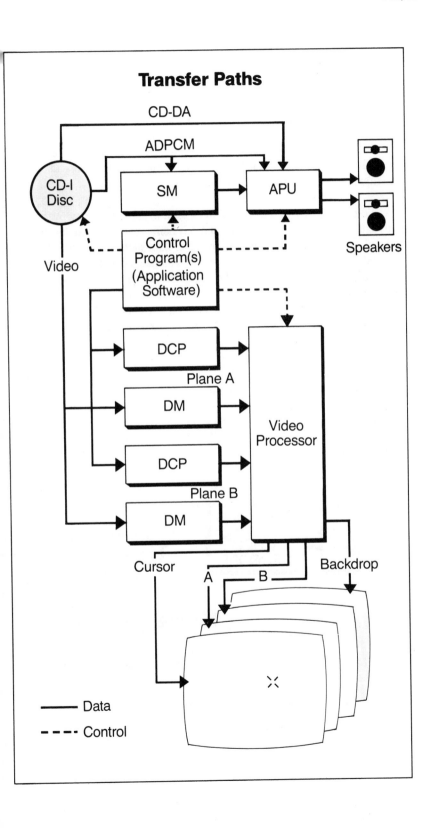

Transfer Paths

CD-DA

ADPCM

CD-I Disc

SM

APU

Speakers

Control Program(s) (Application Software)

Video

DCP

Plane A

DM

Video Processor

DCP

Plane B

DM

Cursor

A   B   Backdrop

—— Data

---- Control

Audio Pathways

Audio can travel along four different routes depending on its source and use. CD-DA is played direct from the disc through the Audio Processing Unit (APU) to the playback system and does not enter the CD-I controller.

Most CD-I audio at A, B or C-Level is played directly from the disc in real-time. Playback is controlled by the CD control unit, which channels digital audio data to the APU for playback.

Audio from the disc is the determining factor in the real-time recovery of all data read from the disc. While audio is being read from one location, the player cannot look elsewhere for other data such as a picture. Thus, sound and pictures required in the same sequence must be interleaved in the data stream. To have an audio sequence with a range of choice for accompanying pictures, the audio must be stored in multiple locations on the disc, interleaved with a new set of pictures at each location. This, in turn, would require a lower audio quality or a slower rate of picture change.

Playback from System Memory

Soundmaps can be loaded into temporary memory from disc or the MPU. Like direct playback from disc, digital sound data is converted to analog signals in the decoder and played through the APU.

Video Pathways

All video images are loaded into RAM before display on the video screen. Sectors of video are interleaved with sectors of audio in the data stream. Video data can be retrieved from the CD disc or synthesized in the MPU before being stored in one of the two Image Stores (RAM).

Image Store (RAM)

From RAM, the video data passes through a decoder which sends it to the appropriate screen plane for display on a monitor or television. The video decoder has two real-time decoders which convert digital video to analog RGB signals in the appropriate resolution. One real-time decoder receives imagery from Image Store 0 (RAM 0) through path 0 which, when decoded, will be passed to the 8-bit image plane supplied by that decoder. The other decoder is supplied by Image Store 1 via Path 1.

The real-time decoders control screen effects by designating the screen area and the contribution of each screen to the overall image.

A dissolve is a simple example of this: a one-second dissolve from a desert scene on Plane A to a camel caravan on Plane B requires the controller to increase the full screen contribution of Plane B from 0 to 100% over one second as it decreases the contribution of Plane A from 100% to 0.

CD-RTOS

At the heart of every computer is its operating system, the program controls all the other software programs and hardware. CD-I has its own Compact Disc-Real-Time Operating System (CD-RTOS), designed specifically for demands of interactive multi-media information management in real-time. It is based on a high-performance operating system called OS-9, which is concisely written in 68000 assembler code. This section summarizes the main features of CD-RTOS. Further details are given in Appendix C.

Organization

The organization of CD-RTOS is shown in the diagram. At the top is the application program which communicates with the CD-RTOS kernel through various libraries. Housekeeping modules are connected to the kernel, and below the kernel are the file managers: the Compact Disc File Manager, Pipe File Manager, Non-volatile RAM File Manager, and the User Communications Manager.

Below the managers are the various drivers, which interface directly with the hardware described above. The drivers allow for differences between hardware from different manufacturers.

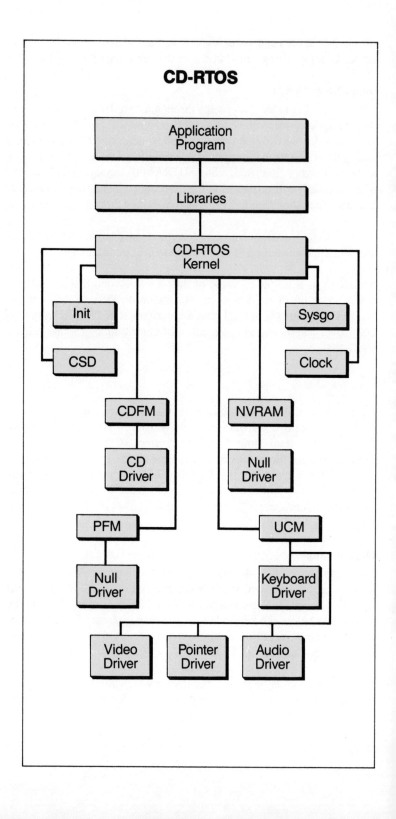

THE KERNEL

The kernel is the heart of CD-RTOS. It provides multi-tasking, handling all task control itself, including task switching and task suspension. It also handles memory management (including the allocation and de-allocation of memory as the application demands), all the interrupts generated in the CD-I player, all the systems service requests, the I/O (input/output) calls and so on which pass through it.

Finally, it handles control between individual tasks and synchronization, a vital task. There are several ways of communicating between tasks: simple software interrupts that the processes can send between each other; events or semaphores; shared memory in the form of data modules; or pipes which allow communication through the I/O system.

Configuration Status Descriptor

The configuration status descriptor (CSD) is an integral part of the CD-I system. Basically, it allows an application to discover what devices are available on the player and information about these devices, such as their capability. There is an entry in the CSD for each device on the system, stored in RAM/ROM with additional parts in non-volatile RAM. It is also possible for the user to configure the machine using the CSD mechanism, perhaps to indicate a choice of control device.

Each CSD entry, known as a device status descriptor, includes four parts: the device type, name, active status (such as whether it is busy), and a set of parameters which are specific for each device.

All the devices in the decoder, including the base case devices, will be represented in the CSD, which will indicate, for example: the capabilities of the video processor (for example, whether it can do high resolution), the audio processor, the NVRAM size and so forth - all of which will be described in the configuration status descriptor.

The CSD also provides information for any extensions or peripherals which may be connected to the decoder - floppy disc, keyboard, printer, modem and so on.

Start-up Procedure

When the CD-I decoder is switched on and a disc inserted, the software performs the start-up procedure. The hardware is initialized, the CD-RTOS kernel is started and the system copyright message is displayed. After that, the boot file is loaded from the disc, or, if there is no boot file, the configuration status descriptor is compiled.

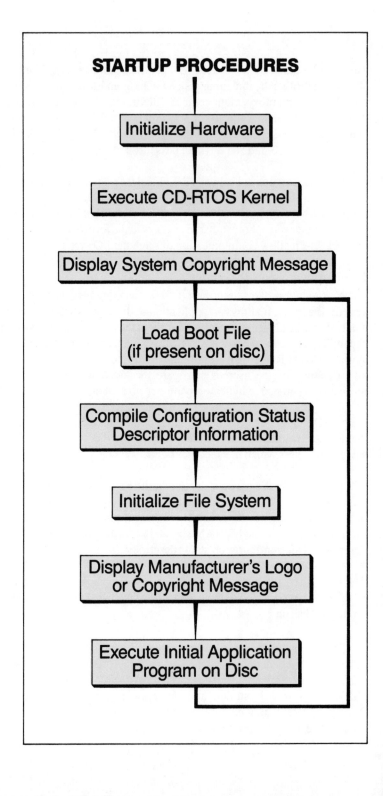

The file system is then initialized. This involves reading the Disc Label and the Path Table which shows the layout of what is on the disc. After that, it may display the manufacturer's label and copyright message, before executing the first application program pointed to by the disc label.

If the user removes the disc and inserts another, this process is repeated from the point indicated in the diagram.

File Protection

The disc file protection mechanism restricts access to certain files: this allows a content provider to protect up to 32 different files or combination of files per disc through access codes. This means a disc can be designed to contain several application programmes, access to which can be individually controlled through separate access codes and licence fees: the customer may buy the disc and pay for one or two applications, with the option of accessing others, for a fee, at a later date.

Each CD-I player has a unique code, in addition to which there is an encryption method in the kernel which will match the player and the access codes to control access to the files.

For example, a disc may contain up to 32 games. When the user purchases the disc he pays a fee for this first game only. Later, he may pay for other games on the same disc and receive an access code which is fed into the CD-I player using the keyboard or pointer. The application must provide the mechanism for carrying this out. (Note that the access code will be different for each application and each player.) In this way the user pays only for the games he wishes to play.

FILE MANAGERS

The file managers are located between the kernel and the drivers and are used to provide the I/O despatching. The main CD-RTOS file managers are: the User Communication Manager (UCM), the Compact Disc File Manager (CDFM) and the Non-Volatile RAM File Manager (NRF).

UCM Video

The User Communications Manager provides software support for the video graphics devices available, the pointer devices, the optional keyboard and audio processor. The UCM video functions support the organization of the two image planes, and the creation and manipulation of multiple images in memory, and provide basic graphics drawing and text functions.

DRAWMAPS: A drawmap is simply an area of memory which can be used by the application to store and manipulate images, either loaded from disc or created using the drawing functions. Drawmaps can have several formats: DYUV and CLUT images are stored as a rectangular array while Run-length images are stored as a list. RGB 5:5:5 requires two drawmaps, one in each memory bank.

Examples of UCM drawmap functions include:

- 'create and close' (used for allocating and de-allocating memory for drawmaps);

- 'copy and exchange', for transferring image data between drawmaps (useful for rectangular updates and for animation);

- 'transparent copy and exchange', similar to 'copy and exchange', except that pixels of specific value are not transferred (also useful for animation purposes).

If a drawmap is larger than full screen size, the display may be scrolled around the larger image. Drawmaps smaller than the screen size may be used to create animation effects: for example, partial updates may be handled as small drawmaps, a succession of which are overwritten in turn onto a larger drawmap. The use of transparency allows a non-rectangular object to be overwritten on a larger drawmap.

GRAPHICS DRAWING: The basic graphics drawing functions are line, rectangle, polyline, circle, ellipse, arc and fills. In addition, text in almost any font style and character shape can be drawn. The graphics drawing parameters include the use of patterns, definition of colors, line size, dash style, fonts, writing modes and clipping region.

Other functions include OR, AND and exclusive OR. In practice these functions operate on multi-colored patterns and drawmaps, encoded as either CLUT or RGB.

REGIONS: Regions may be used to limit the drawing area within drawmaps. In addition, the data which is generated by the regions can be used in the display control program to create mattes for special effects.

Regions can be created in several basic shapes: rectangles, polygons, wedges, ellipses, and so forth. In addition, these basic shapes can be combined through region operations. Regions may also be used to clip drawmaps: so, for example, that part of a line which lies outside the region can be clipped.

DISPLAY CONTROL PROGRAM: The UCM provides functions to load the display control program which was described above.

UCM Audio

The audio part of the user communications manager controls the flow of ADPCM sound and control signals from the MPU or memory to the ADPCM decoder. It supports the creation from the application, specific sounds and allows the sounds to be manipulated in memory as well as to support the hardware mixing, panning and attenuation capabilities of the audio processing unit. It manipulates soundmaps, which are basically a memory area that an application can use to preload data from the disc. Soundmap manipulation functions allow different types of audio data to be mixed together before they are sent to the audio processor.

UCM User Interface

The UCM also supports the X/Y pointer devices and optional keyboard, and provides functions for the application to read data from the keyboard and the position indicated by the X/Y pointer device.

Compact Disc File Manager (CDFM)

The Compact Disc File Manager converts high-level commands from the application to device driver commands. It provides access to and interpretation of the disc file system, carries out any necessary access protection and schedules the disc access.

It may be that the application which is running requires multi-tasking, or that more than one application is running on the system: the CDFM schedules these accesses to the disc so that access requests are processed in the order in which they appear on the disc - which may not be the order in which they appear in time.

This process works something like a lift, which from the ground floor to the top, stopping not in the order in which the passengers indicated their individual floors, but as the floors themselves appear.

The following service requests are processed by CDFM:

- Open Path to Specified File

- Change User's Default Directories

- Change Current File Position Pointer (Seek)

- Read Data From File

- Get Specified Status Information

- Set Status Information
- Perform Special Function
- Close a File

Note that Seek allows movement within a data file, real-time record or real-time file, to skip over certain real-time records in the program.

NV-RAM File Manager (NRF)

The NV-RAM File Manager provides a filing system for the application to write files to the NV-RAM, through a simple version of the Random Block file manager available on OS-9 for magnetic discs. It provides a basic directory structure with only one NV-RAM directory and no sub-directories. File names may be generated by the application, providing there is no duplication.

Since the amount of memory is limited (a minimum of 8K bytes for the base case decoder), the application must use this memory very efficiently.

DRIVERS

The device drivers provide the necessary interface between the file managers and the devices themselves. The drivers will take account of any differences in devices from different manufacturers so that a standard interface is presented to the manager and therefore to the application. The drivers will handle all of the low-level functions which the file managers provide to the application.

SYNCHRONIZATION AND CONTROL

Synchronization, which co-ordinates audio and video effects in the final presentation, can be achieved in several ways:

- A software timer, which can be instructed to generate a timed signal.
- A user input, which can also generate a signal.
- A signal from another application, which is running concurrently.
- A trigger bit, an end of record bit or end of file bits in the sub-header of sectors.
- Full buffer signal from one of the Play Control List buffers.
- End of the transfer of requested records.

Control of the flow of data through the system is achieved using the Play Control Structure, while synchronization can be achieved using the trigger settings in sectors and the Real-Time Control Area, both described below.

Play Control Structure

Real-time files typically contain interleaved sectors of audio, video and program-related data. The Play System Call used to play real-time files selects sectors by file number, channel number and data type (audio, video or program-related). It also controls the destination of the data through the Play Control Blocks and Play Control Lists, and signals the application software whenever a specific event occurs in the program.

At the heart of Play System Call is the Play Control Block, which provides the means to de-interleave the data as it arrives in the player, and store audio, video and program related-data in the appropriate parts of the memory. The Play Control Block points to the audio, video and data Play Control Lists.

Audio data may, of course, be sent directly to the audio processor or to the memory as a soundmap. The Play Control Block provides the channel selection mask to indicate which audio sectors are to be placed in memory and which should be directed to the audio output.

The Audio Play Control List points to the soundmap to which the audio data should be directed. Similarly, the Video Play Control List points to the appropriate drawmap, and the Data Play Control List to the area where the data is to be directed in memory.

Real-Time Control Area

The Data Play Control List buffer includes text and control data, the latter usually in a Real-Time Control Area (RTCA) which is interpreted by the Real-Time Record Interpreter (RTRI). This is used to control the real-time playback and synchronization of a real-time file.

There is a Real-Time Control Area at the beginning of each real-time record; the RTRI decodes the function codes within the RTCA for both the audio and video effects and provides synchronization information.

The Real-Time Control Area contains a number of commands which are used to control the playing of real-time records, the loading of audio and video data, the manipulation and display of drawmaps, and the output of audio data.

It is also used to synchronize audio and video, and contains facilities for user interaction. The commands in the Real-Time Control Area can be executed in sequence or in parallel or, more likely, a combination of the two.

The RTRI is a truly multi-tasking interpreter which can handle a large number of parallel tasks. This is necessary to ensure that data can be loaded from disc and displayed for output to the audio processor while inputting user responses.

The RTCA is a genuine real-time programming facility that provides all the structures with which programmers are familiar, and is also capable of multi-tasking.

InVision

A series of efficient and easy-to-use tools are a useful addition to any language designed to be used by application programmers. An object-orientated multi-media user interface called InVision was been developed for CD-RTOS. While alternative User Interfaces and associated programming tools will no doubt emerge, InVision is the first of its kind.

InVision is designed for the programmer in the development of CD-I applications as well as the actual user of a CD-I player. The user will normally be presented by a version of the InVision user interface modules adapted to the specific CD-I disc by the programming team who developed the application.

However, InVision is more than a User Interface. It contains a series of tools and functions designed to integrate into CD-RTOS. These collected into three main modules:

- Visual Shell: the only part of InVision that the user will actually see, this essentially forms the control panel of the CD-I player.

- Presentation Support Library: a collection of sub-routines intended to simplify the task of manipulating the display, and obtaining input from the user.

- Display Manager: a CD-RTOS sub-routine module for the UCM file manager which provides access to the video, audio, pointer and keyboard driver routines.

Further details of InVision can be found in Appendix C.

APPENDIX A: TECHNICAL SPECIFICATION SUMMARY

The following technical specification information is provided for your information, and has been used for the calculations and other technical statements made in this book.

Units of Measurement

1 Mega byte = 1,024 kilo bytes
1 Kilo byte = 1,024 bytes
1 Sector   = 2,352 bytes with headers and synch info.
                = 2,048 bytes (Form 1) user data
                = 2,324 bytes (Form 2) user data
                = 2,336 bytes (CD-DA)

Disc Capacity

650M bytes

Disc Transfer Rate

75 sectors/sec = 150k bytes/sec (Form 1)
                    = 170.2k bytes/sec (Form 2)
                    = 171.1k bytes/sec (CD-DA)

N.B. Above is useful data rate, less headers, etc.

Screen Resolution

NTSC: 360 x 240 pixels = 86,400/1024   = 84.4k bytes
PAL : 384 x 280 pixels = 107,520/1024 = 105k bytes

Typical Values

1 DYUV natural image picture = 85k bytes NTSC (105k bytes PAL)
Partial update of 1/3 by 1/3 of screen (= 1/9 of screen area)
                        = approx. 8.5k bytes = 10%

So with a data rate of 170.2 at 15 frames per second you can have 170.2/15 = 11.35k bytes per frame, based on either partial update of a DYUV natural image picture, or a full screen update of RL-7 CLUT cartoon picture

N.B. Partial update can be improved to some 50% of the screen area by software techniques.

1 second CD-DA sound   = 171.1k bytes

1 second Level A Stereo   = 85.1k bytes
              Mono   = 42.5k bytes

1 second Level B Stereo   = 42.5k bytes
              Mono   = 21.3k bytes

1 second Level C Stereo   = 21.3k bytes
              Mono   = 10.6k bytes

Max theorectical playing time   = 74 mins 33 secs
practical playing time (CD-DA & form2 CD-I)   = 72 mins
practical playing time (CD-ROM & form1 CD-I)   = 65 mins

Disc design must take the following factors into account:

- disc storage capacity

- transfer channel capacity

- system RAM allocation

- microprocessor load

The whole disc can contain:

7,830 DYUV NTSC natural image pictures (650M bytes = 650x1024/85)
6,340 DYUV PAL natural image pictures (650M bytes = 650x1024/105)

or

65 minutes of cartoon animation plus Level C mono sound

or

17 hours 18 mins of Level C mono sound (16 channels x 65 mins)

or

100 million words (150,000 pages of text)

APPENDIX B: GLOSSARY OF TERMS

absolute disc addresses The location of a given sector on the disc in minutes, seconds and sectors, contained in the header of the sector.

absolute RGB coding See direct RGB coding

absolute RGB components Every color can be represented as the sum of different proportions of the three primary colors, red, (R), green (G) and blue (B). In absolute RGB encoding, every pixel is represented by its R, G and B components. These are values which, on presentation to suitable digital to analog converters will give the correct voltages required by the red, green and blue guns of a cathode ray tube to produce the color of the pixel on the display screen.

absolute sector address The address part of the sector header field. Its value corresponds to the absolute disc address.

absolute time In CD-DA, the total time a disc has been playing. Included in the subcode and thus available for display during playback.

access The process of locating information in a data store.

access controller A CD-I player component that takes drawmaps from RAM and loads them to the video decoder.

access key The key supplied by a content provider to allow access to a group of files protected by a file protection code.

access protection The method of preventing unauthorised access to specific data of a confidential nature, stored on a disc.

active line scan period The time taken by the electron beam of a cathode ray tube to move across the visible part of a line on the screen.

active display The contents of a video memory currently being displayed, as opposed to screen contents being held in memory for later display if needed.

active regions Areas on a display screen which respond when indicated by a pointing device/cursor under user control. Used for user input in interactive systems such as CD-I.

adaptive delta pulse code modulation A technique for converting analog audio into digital audio in any CD-I level. Delta modulation assumes close correlation between successive samples. It cannot accurately express large transients in an audio signal, because the correlation between successive samples is too low. Adaptive delta pulse code modulation is a variant of delta modulation in which the quantization steps are adapted to the dynamic amplitude variation. This adaptation can include a temporary switch to PCM. See delta modulation, pulse code modulation.

ADPCM See adaptive delta pulse code modulation.

address of path table The block address of the first block of the system path table.

ADPCM decoder Device which converts CD-I audio sector encoded data to 2's Complement 16-bit PCM encoded audio.

album A set of discs.

American Standard Code for Information Interchange (ASCII) A standard data transmission code designed to achieve compatibility between data devices.

analog versus digital In analog systems, natural sound and images are converted into corresponding variations in electrical voltages or currents. The resulting electronic signals vary according to the original sound or image in a completely linear fashion. These signals aree then processed in various ways, such as making and playing a record or tape, or transmitting the signal for reception at a remote receiver. The signal is then amplified and reproduced locally. The same lineare technique was used in the past in the telephone system, for transferring the spoken voice from one telephone to another.

One of the major disadvantages of analog technology is the occurence of noise and distortion. Noise occurs in the form of disturbances to the original signal caused by extraneous effects in the electronic circuitry used in the analog system. Distortion arises when any part of the signal processing system fails to represent the original signal accurately. Noise and distortion in an analog system are virtually impossible to remove, as they aree superimposed on the signal information itself.
The concepts behind digital systems were first developed for telephony systems, where increasing demand for long distance communications brought attention to the need to reduce or eliminate noise and interference signals. The development of the semiconductor, and with it the mass

produced computer components now commonplace in the area of professional electronics, brought digital technology into the consumer area.

Digital circuitry works on the principle of defining all signals as a range of specific values or numbers, rather than by a continually variable voltage or current. In digital recording, the original signal is captured, and converted into a sequence of values, each representing the instantaneous level of the signal at a given moment. By repeating these samples at a fast enough frequency, or sampling rate, all the changes in the original sound or picture can be accurately recorded.

animation The art or process of synthesizing apparent mobility of inanimate objects or drawings. See CLUT animation.

appliance controller A dedicated circuit, between a computer and an associated appliance, through which the computer controls the appliance.

applications software A computer program written for a specific user application.

ASCII See American Standard Code for Information Interchange.

aspect ratio The width to height ratio of an image or a pixel.

audio block A block of audio information in CD-I format.

audio block field bytes 2304 bytes of data in a CD-I audio sector. The audio block is further subdivided into 18 sound groups of 128 bytes each. The sound groups have to be encoded in sequential order.

audio channel Audio data from one source. Up to 16 audio channels can be encoded in a CD-I track.

audio data (1) Audio information expressed in digital form. (2) In CD-DA, multiplexed and pulse code modulated stereo information with CIRC and subcode added. (3) In CD-I, audio information encoded in accordance with the CD-I specification.

audio functions User Communications Manager functions which are concerned with the maintenance and manipulation of ADPCM sound.

audio mixing control unit Adjusts the volume and balance distribution of audio information.

audio processing unit Converts digitally coded audio information to the 'left' and 'right' analog outputs. Also includes an Audio Mixing Control Unit.

audio sector A data field containing audio data.

audio sector data format The data field of an audio sector comprises a sub-header, an audio data block of 2304 bytes and 20 bytes with value 0.

audio quality level See sound quality level.

audio track A CD-DA track with information encoded as 16-bit wide 2's-Complement numbers. A separately addressable section of a CD-DA disc, normally carrying a self-contained piece of music. Has a minimum duration of 4 seconds and a maximum duration of 72 minutes. One CD-DA disc can contain between one and 99 audio tracks, but the total disc playing time cannot exceed 72 minutes.

authoring The work involved in producing the software for a CD-I application, from the initial concept to the recording of the master tape required for the disc mastering process. Authoring embraces:

- Encoding the required audio, video, text and binary data into CD-I data formats.

- Developing and producing the application software which operates on, uses or accesses the encoded CD-I data as required by the application.

- Structuring the encoded CD-I data and application software into the disc label, files and records corresponding to the access and playback requirements of the application.

- Verifying and validating the application so produced via, at the least, a CD-I disc/base case combination.

authoring process In CD-I, the process of developing and producing the complete software for an application. It involves (a) Designing the program content by creating the story board. (b) Creating and capturing data, and preparing it for use. (c) Developing the program that will appear on the disc. (d) Simulating and testing the program in practice. (e) Preparing the final master tape.

The first step in the process is the creation of an overall program design, or story board. This is critical to the success of the project, as it defines not only the type of basic material or data required for the video, audio and text/graphics components, but also the interrelationships between them. The concept of interactivity, in which the response of the system depends upon the response of the user at each stage of the program, means that the whole project stands or falls upon the 'what happens then' response of the overall CD-I system. This involves both the player and the disc, as well as the user. The key to this action-and-response relationship must be clearly defined in the story board design phase if the program is to be sucessful.

It is unlikely that the story board will get the design right at the first attempt. One of the essentials of CD-I program design is step-by-step evaluation of results, leading to redesign and re-evaluation in an on-going interactive process. With both the application data and the application software on the disc, (all the information on a single medium),

There is no opportunity to correct errors once the disc is released for replication and sale.

So simulation, evaluation, validation, testing and, where needed, revision, are essential steps in every phase of the CD-I authoring process. And the controlling mechanism for this process is the story board.

Based on a first issue of the story board, design work proceeds along two parallel paths. The first involves content collection; the assembly and production, when needed, of the video, audio, text and graphics information required by the story board. This basic information may be in either digital or analog form, or may have to be generated from scratch. Continuing along this first path, the collected data is tested and evaluated at each phase for correctness, and for the right balance of quality versus disc capacity. While Compact Disc-Digital Audio sound takes 100% of the information channel from the disc to the player, monaural speech takes only 6% of this capacity, leaving 94% for other information - video, text/graphics, application software or indexing information. The choice of a balance between quality and data bandwidth is a key element in program design.

Once satisfactory, data is encoded and compressed to CD-I format, and prepared as data files onto a disc simulator. This is built around a large capacity read/write store (typically hard discs are used, with a capacity in excess of 1200 megabytes) and is part of the authoring studio equipment).

The second path involves the development and testing of the application software and user interfaces needed to interact with the data used in the program.

Each stage of this application software development is testd on its own, and slowly integrated and synchronized with the relevant data as it in turn is collected.

In this way, the integration and synchronization of each portion of the program is tested to prove it works as defined in the storyboard, before integration into the next level of the design.

And once completed the first time, the program is then tested, revised, and retested on the disc simulator until the overall design and balance has been proven.

Only at this stage can thought be given to transferring the total program to the disc replication facility.

authoring system In CD-I, a general term for the equipment, in hardware and software, needed for authoring CD-I discs.

authoring tool A computer programming aid used in authoring.

auto-play, auto-play mode In CD-I, the play sequence of a CD-I disc when no user input is given, or when the CD-I player is so instructed by the user. Used for demonstration or training of the disc application, or for general information sequences.

auxiliary data field In CD-ROM and CD-I the last 288 bytes of a sector, either used for extra error detection and correction (mode 1 and form 1) or available as user data area (mode 2 and form 2). See mode 1, mode 2, form 1, form 2.

backdrop The background image plane that is displayed when all other planes are made transparent.

background plane Synonymous with backdrop.

base case disc In CD-I, a hypothetical disc that can exercise all the capabilities of a Base Case system. See Base Case system.

base case See Base Case system.

base case system The minimum characteristics of a system that may bear the CD-I name.

BER See bit error rate.

bit error rate A measure of the capacity of a data medium to store or transmit bits without errors. Expressed as the average number of bits the medium can handle with only one bit in error. CD-ROM and CD-I, which employ three layers of error detection and correction (CIRC and EDC/ECC) have a bit error rate of 10^{-18} (one error per 10^{18} bits).

bit inversion A random error causing erroneous read-out of a bit, a 1 becoming 0, and vice versa.

bit-mapped display A screen display in which each pixel location corresponds to a unique memory location whose contents determine the intensity and color values of the pixel.

bit map The process by which a picture is built up on a pixel- by-pixel basis.

bit mapped text Specific characters generated by bit maping.

bits per sample The number of bits used to express the numerical value of a digitized sample.

block In CD-ROM and CD-I, the user-data portion of a sector.

block address A 32-bit integer that is converted to an absolute disc address to access information on the disc.

boot file Optional File on a CD-I disc containing a program to be executed when the CD-I disc is first mounted. It can be used to add or replace Operating System modules in the Base Case system.

boot identifier Identifies the operating system which supports this boot.

boot record An optional record on a CD-I disc that specifies where the Boot File is on the disc. The contents of the Boot File is loaded into memory when the disc is first mounted.

border The area outside a visual image which is reduced below the full screen size.

burst error The corruption of a sequence of bits caused e.g. by a read error, tracking error or electromagnetic interference.

CARIN CAR Information and Navigation system developed by Philips for computerized on-the-road route planning and route following, using digital maps recorded on CD-ROM discs, in association with navigation sensors.

cartesian coordinate system A system for locating a point in a plane by specifying its distance from two axes which intersect at right angles.

cartoon-style image An image containing significant areas of the same color which can be efficiently Run-Length coded.

CAV See constant angular velocity.

CD See Compact Disc.

CD-DA See Compact Disc Digital Audio.

CD-DA controller/decoder The hardware needed to play a CD-DA or CD-I disc and to decode the information coming from the disc, either in the form of CD-DA audio information or other information passed to the digital output port of the controller/ decoder.

CD-DA data Data encoded according to the CD-DA specification.

CD-DA track A track on a Compact Disc containing music encoded according to the CD-Digital Audio specification.

CD device driver The lowest software level to handle CD drives. The only software to communicate directly with the CD control unit, it resides in ROM on a CD-I player.

CD-disc master A CD master disc, produced by exposing a photosensitive coating on a glass substrate to a laser beam. The laser is modulated by the digital program information from the CD-tape master, together with the subcode, which is generated during the disc mastering process from the subcode cue code, also on the CD tape master. The exposed coating is developed, covered with a silver coating and nickel plated to form a 'metal father' recording mould. See CD Mastering, Metal Father.

CD drive The drive mechanism portion of any CD player.

CDFM See Compact Disc file manager.

CD graphics In CD-DA, a technique for generating text, still pictures or animated graphics, related to the music. The graphic information is recorded in subcode channels R-W. Presently used in Japan only. Not related to the graphics facilities of CD-I.

CD-I See Compact Disc-Interactive.

CD-I channel The main channel of a CD-I track corresponding to the specifications of CD-ROM, mode 2 and the CD-I logical and physical formats.

CD-I disc design See authoring process.

CD-Interactive digital audio In CD-I, there is a requirement to have audio data on disc at a number of distinct quality levels. These quality levels are equivalent to LP record quality, FMradio quality, AM radio quality, and telephone quality. Further, CD-Digital Audio information can also be played on CD-I equipment.
In addition to CD-DA sound in 16-bit pulse code modulation (PCM) format, CD-I audio data is also coded in 8- or 4-bit Adaptive Delta Pulse Code Modulation (ADPCM) formats. This technique is chosen as a way of coding sound more efficiently than for CD-DA, such that 50% or less of the total data rate is occupied by stereo audio information. At least 50% of the data rate can therefore be used for other purposes, principally the transfer of visual information. The Hi Fi music mode uses an 8-bit word size and a sampling rate of 37.8 kHz in order to take full advantage of the form 2 sector space of 2324 Bytes, while remaining the highest usable integral fraction of 44.1 kHz (i.e. the 16-bit PCM sampling rate). Hi Fi music mode is equivalent in quality to a high-quality LP played for the first time. In order to use the same coding technique to span the requirement for various audio levels and still maintain optimal quality by proper post-filtering, the word size of the first level is reduced from 8 bits to 4 bits to give the Mid Fi music mode. This is equivalent to FM broadcast quality sound as broadcast from the studio, and offers a maximum of 4 stereo or 8 mono channels in parallel as opposed to the 2 stereo or 4 mono channels available in the Hi Fi music mode. To achieve a further reduction in data rate, and thereby increase the number of audio channels to 8 stereo or 16 mono, the sampling rate is reduced by half to 18.9 kHz. This results in the speech mode quality, which is equivalent to AM broadcast quality sound as broadcast from the studio.

It should be noted that a channel as described above is equivalent to some 70 minutes of uninterrupted playing time. Multiple channels can only be played with a 1-4 second gap between them. This gap is due to the fact that the laser read-out mechanism must be repositioned back to the beginning of the disc.
An alternative way of using the channels is as a sequence of up to 16 parallel channels of audio information. These channels could tell the same story but in different languages, for example, so that the user could switch from one language to another instantly at any time. This last case moves away from the question of what is on the disc alone, to the question of how that information can be used in a CD-I system.

Audio information from the disc can reach the user in three different ways. (1) From the disc directly to the 16-bit PCM decoder, and out through the audio Hi Fi system as CD-DA sound. (2) From the disc directly through the ADPCM and PCM decoders and the Hi Fi system as ADPCM sounds. (3) From disc into a microprocessor-controlled random access memory, where it can either be held awaiting its singular or repeated use whenever a certain event occurs (for example a ball bouncing on the screen, which must be accompanied by the appropriate sound), or it can be slightly altered as a function of different events and then sent under microprocessor control through the ADPCM and PCM decoders and out to the Hi Fi system. This latter approach allows for audio interactivity with a quality that has been unachievable in the past. See adaptive delta pulse code modulation, delta modulation, pulse code modulation.

CD-Interactive digital video In CD-I, there is a requirement for various video quality levels to offer a choice of resolution and color depths to satisfy various pictorial functions in the applications. Three resolution levels are defined: the best achievable resolution for pictures on present normal TV receivers (normal resolution); the best achievable resolution for characters displayed on present normal TV receivers (double resolution); the best achievable resolution with the coming enhanced-quality TV sets (high resolution). As for color depth, the quality necessary depends on the type of image that is being handled. Natural stills use YUV (luminance and color signals) coding for an equivalent of 24-bit total color depth per pixel, quality graphics employ Color Look-Up Tables (CLUTs), and user-manipulated graphics use direct RGB coding.

A key requirement is that the disc must be compatible regardless of where it is purchased and on which system is is used, i.e. playback should be independent of the particular TV standard. Given these and other similarities and differences, CD-I video requirements are translated into specifications related to three areas:

- display resolution
- picture coding
- visual effects.

CD-I systems will work with, and CD-I disc contents will be displayable on, normal TV sets. The video coding adopted conforms, as far as possible, with prevailing industry conventions relating to color depth, visual effects and studio world considerations, while remaining independent of the TV standard (525/625 lines).

The starting point for the specification of resolution, in addition to 525/625-line display systems compatibility is to ensure the readability of text, the undistorted shape of graphics, and the full screen view of natural pictures on display. To do this, two sets of resolution areas are defined; one as a safety area for text and graphics, the other a full screen for natural and animated pictures. Moreover, three disc formats are defined:

- a 525-line format for NTSC studios

- a 625-line format for PAL studios

- a 525/625-line-compatible format that can be used in the international market to satisfy all compatibility requirements.

Each format is usable on each display system with, however, a quality penalty. The basic numbers for normal resolution, i.e. the best resolution visible on a non-interlaced TV, are 384 x 280 pixels for full screen and 320 x 210 pixels for the safety area. For maximum readability of characters on a normal TV display, the double resolution mode is defined.

This mode has twice the number of horizontal pixels as the normal resolution mode. For future programs, but still keeping in line with the data rate limitations of Compact Discs, a high-resolution mode is defined as twice the horizontal and twice the vertical resolution of the normal resolution mode, giving 768 x 560 pixels for full screen and 640 x 420 pixels for the safety area. This is also consistent with high-resolution or 525/625-line-compatible digital TV.

The net distortion is at most 7% for a 525 or 625-line disc on a 625 or 525-line decoder, respectively, and 3.6% for compatible discs on 525 or 625-line decoders.

This is a considerable improvement on the 20% distortion obtained when NTSC (525 line) material is transferred to PAL (625 line) systems for viewing. Also, it relates quite favourably to the fact that the eye can only resolve, at best, distortions of 5% if the original and the distorted object are side-by-side on the same screen; if they are not side-by-side the eye can only resolve, at best, distortions of 10% for objects of a familiar shape (e.g. circle, square etc). Even these low CD-I distortions will be reduced to zero when real-time pixel manipulation is added to CD-I equipment.

As far as picture coding is concerned, three target areas are defined by CD-I applications:

- natural pictures
- graphics:
  ○ complex graphics, minimum download time
  ○ complex graphics, locally created
- animation

In all cases, it is necessary to use compression techniques to decrease the amount of data required for a given picture, and thus the loading time and memory storage requirements. By using compression, the achievable update speed, the number of images that can be put on a disc, and the number of video 'channels' available per unit are all increased. Clearly, video coding needs to be simple so that the decoding can be affordable, and it must also be capable of being performed in real time while still maintaining image quality.

The compression techniques chosen are:

- 1-dimensional delta YUV (DYUV) for natural pictures
- direct RGB coding for high-quality end- user manipulated graphics
- Color Look-Up Table (CLUT) for graphics and fast update and manipulation
- 1-dimensional Run-Length coding combined with CLUT for animation.

Each of these techniques gives optimal performance in the area of use for which they were chosen. In particular, with DYUV coding there is no visible difference between the compressed and original pictures. Four different sizes of CLUT, two used with Run-Length coding, offer an efficient trade-off between the number of colors needed and the rate of change required. If pictures coded in DYUV or CLUT graphics are intermingled with audio data in speech mode quality, for example to explain their content or to enhance a story, then 3 full-screen pictures(normal resolution mode compatible format) can be displayed every 2 seconds while the audio is playing. Moreover, for full-screen animations like cartoons, real motion is achievable with the Run-Length compression coding specified.

The data rate of the CD-I data channel is not high enough for visual effects such as cuts and wipes to be performed in the full motion video data stream (as is done in movies, for example). Furthermore, for interactive use it is desirable to have not only more channel space (for more effective use of CD-I), but also the ability to vary the visual effects used on the same picture data as a function of end-user activity or computer software state. Visual effects are therefore approached at a higher level, e.g. via control functions in the data stream, rather than embedding them uniquely in a moving data stream.

As far as operations on a single visual plane are concerned, CD-I at the basic system level will be capable at least of:

- cuts

- smooth x,y scrolling

- efficient updating of any part of a visual field independent of the contents of the rest of the visual field

- CLUT animation

- trading-off picture resolution against visual data thoughput, for a constant visual field size.

The overlaying of images is based on the ability to have at least one hardware cursor plane available, one, two or three independent full-screen full-picture visual planes available, and one backdrop plane available for use with external video at a pixel level. These plane combinations allow CD-I to be used for a variety of applications as encountered in multi-cell film work, e.g. in animations, in games-like manipulations of objects over objects, or with a background over a foreground. In CD-I, the control of overlays is done by a transparency bit for the pixels of the cursor, and also the RGB plane. As for the use of the CLUT, a color key is used to control the overlay of such planes, while for DYUV the pixel-wise overlaying of regions under well-defined transparency/translucency conditions is used.

The final point concerning CD-I visual is that of operations between two visual planes. There are rwo main categories of such operations:

- wipes, and

- dissolves or fades.

Wipes and dissolves are well known in the film and video industries as well as, in a simpler form, in professional slide shows. They are very important in maintaining an attractive presentation potential in CD-I for both stills and moving picture sequences. These effects, together with the other visual effects described, bring CD-I as close as possible to the present passive video world, while at the same time allowing for interactivity via either end-user or software control of visual information.

This multi-faceted control of visual content and visual information flow as perceived and influenced by the end-user makes CD-I potentially the richest artistic medium ever created. See color look-up table, delta YUV, direct RGB coding and Run-Length coding.

CD-I physical format   The way in which data is stored on a CD-I disc.

CD-I physical sector   Directly addressable sector in a CD-I disc numbered consecutively beginning at zero.

CD-I sector   A unit of data of 2352 bytes.

CD-I system   A real-time system capable of playing CD-I discs.

CD-I track   A data track containing only mode 2 sectors conforming to the CD-I specification.

CD-master tape   A master tape for Compact Disc, containing all the program information in the required digital format, and organized in the correct relationship.   See CD mastering. Compare CD-tape master.

CD-mastering   In gramophone record production, mastering is the process of recording the information from a master tape on to the master disc.   This same basic procedure applies to all Compact Discs (CD-Digital Audio, CD-Video, CD-ROM and CD-I) but with two major differences:

- an additional 'pre-mastering' stage is required to arrange and encode the information in the required Compact Disc format, including CIRC error detection and correction coding, subcode insertion and eight-to-fourteen modulation.

- the recording is 'cut' by exposing a rotating master disc with a photo-sensitive coating to a laser beam modulated by the signal from the CD Tape Master, as it traverses the disc.

In keeping with the microscopic dimensions associated with CD recording, the photosensitive coating is only one-tenth of a micron thick. It is deposited by centrifuging on an optically ground and polished glass disc to form a 'resist master'.

After exposure, controlled photographic development produces a pattern of pits in the photoresist.   To capture this pattern, and thus create a CD Glass Master Disc, silver is evaporated onto the pit pattern.

From the glass master, replication moulds are made along conventional lines by nickel plating and discs are fabricated by injection or compression moulding. But the microscopic dimensions and the requirement of optical read-out have demanded new materials, processes and techniques for stringent quality control.

CD-ROM See Compact Disc-Read-Only Memory.

CD-RTOS See Compact-Disc Real-time Operating System.

CD-RTOS kernel The nucleus of CD-RTOS which is responsible for service request processing, memory management, system initialization, multitasking, input/output management and exception and interrupt processing.

CD-tape master The tape used to produce the CD-disc master; a CD master tape with subcode cue code added. See CD mastering, cue code.

CD track A separately-addressable section of a Compact Disc, normally carrying a self-contained piece of information.

CD-Video Optical recording system extending the CD-DA standard with analog video. Discs may be 12 cm CDV singles, 20 cm EP (extended play) or 30 cm LP (long play) sizes. CD-Video is compatible with the earlier LaserVision standard, so that CD- Video players can play LaserVision discs, of both CLV and CAV types.

CDV See CD-Video.

CD-Video player Device specifically designed to play CD-Video and CD-DA discs. If provided with a digital output and control interface, can also be used in conjunction with a suitable signal processor, to read CD-ROM or CD-I discs. See also omni player.

CD-V single 12 cm CD-Video disc carrying up to 6 minutes of video with digital stereo or 2-channel sound, plus 20 minutes of CD-DA sound.

channel Data blocks within a real-time record can be labelled according to logical 'channels' which can be selected in real time. It is by selecting these channels that the user can change audio, video and text sources during the playing of a real-time record.

channel number A number assigned to pieces of information contained in the real-time record to facilitate the selection of such information.

chroma key See color key.

chrominance Information on hue and saturation (vividness) of an image. Expressed as U and V signals. Compare luminance.

CIRC See Cross-Interleaved Reed-Solomon Code.

clipping In computer graphics, to remove parts of a display that lie outside a selected area. In signal processing, a restriction on the peak amplitude of a waveform.

CLUT See color look-up table

CLUT animation In CD-I, a technique used to impart motion to graphic objects by repeatedly changing the data in the color look-up table. For CLUT coded images, the 256 values in the CLUT control the colors of the entire image, therefore, some simple animation effects are possible simply by redefining some or all of the CLUT contents as a function of time.

CLV See constant linear velocity.

color look-up table A table containing all the colors which may be used in a particular picture. Each entry is an absolute RGB value. The picture may then be encoded using the table addresses rather than the absolute values.

combi player A CD-Video player.

Compact Disc System for reproduction of high-density digital data from an optical disc. Originally conceived as a medium for high-fidelity music reproduction, for which Compact Disc-Digital Audio is now an accepted world standard. Because of the very high disc data storage capacity, Compact Disc is now being applied as a text/data medium for electronic publishing (CD-ROM) and a multiple-function (audio/video/text/data) medium for interactive programs (CD-I). See Compact Disc-Digital Audio, Compact Disc-Interactive and Compact Disc-Read Only Memory.

Compact Disc-Digital Audio Developed jointly by Philips and Sony, and launched in October 1982, Compact Disc-Digital Audio has revolutionized high fidelity recording with its pure sound reproduction, small size and immunity from surface scratching.

The Compact Disc system records music, in the form of digital data, onto a light but robust 12 cm diameter disc, thereby virtually eliminating the problems of dynamic range, background noise, wow and flutter, and other sound disturbances common to earlier sound recording systems. 32-bit analog-to-digital conversion at a sampling rate of 44.1 kHz., in conjunction with CIRC (Cross Interleaved Reed-Solomon Code) error correction and EFM (Eight-to-Fourteen Modulation) a reproducable bandwidth of 10 Hz to 20 kHz within 0.2 dB, a signal to noise ratio of over 100 dB, a signal to noise ratio of over 100 dB, a dynamic range of over 95 dB and imperceptible wow and flutter.

But the feature that distinguishes Compact Disc from other audio recording systems is the fact that it is based on optical recording technology. Optical recording was invented in the Philips Company's research laboratories in Eindhoven, Holland in the late 1960s, and has formed the basis of a range of optical discs products.

The principle behind optical recording is the use of a small laser to burn minute pits in an optically flat surface which is enclosed in a transparent sandwich disc construction. For playback the recorded surface is illuminated with a lower power laser. The light beam is concentrated onto the protected recording surface as the disc is rotated. Light is reflected from the recording surface, and passed to a photo sensor. The amount of light reflected from the disc surface changes depending on whether or not the beam is passing over a hole or pit made during the recording process.

The pits, between 0,9 micron and 3.3 micron long and 0.6 micron wide, are recorded on a spiral track at a pitch of 1.6 micron, sixty times finer than the pitch of an LP record. The track is approximately 5 km long. The music recorded in a normal recording studio is encoded into the CD-DA format and used to drive a recording laser to produce a master disc. Mechanical stamper discs are produced from the original master, and copy discs are then pressed in quantity from these stampers in a specially developed replication process.

The high recording density achievable with optical recording techniques results in over one hour of high quality sound recorded on one side of the disc, the other side being used only for the disc label. CD-DA discs are designed for playback at a constant linear velocity. This means that the speed at which the track is scanned by the laser pickup is a constant 1.25 metres/sec. As a result, the speed of rotation of the disc changes as the disc is played. Play starts at the inside of the recording track, and runs outwards. As the music is played, the rotational speed of the disc drops from some 500 rpm at the beginning of the disc, to some 200 rps at the end. Apart from the main data channel via which the hi fi music is stored, an additional 8 sub-channels, with a much lower data capacity are also available for control and display purposes. These sub-channels, known as P, Q and R through W, are generally available to the recording studio. However, apart from the P and Q sub-channel, little use is made of these sub-channels in practice. While the R through W channels have in fact been specified for a simple graphics application, no sub-channel graphics decoders have as yet become generally available on the market. The disc surface is divided into three main portions. The lead-in area at the centre or start of the disc, the program area and the lead-out area at the outside of the disc. In the lead-in area, the Q sub-channel is used to store details of the contents of the disc. Up to 99 separate music tracks can be specified. A single track has a minimum duration of 4 seconds, and a maximum duration of 72 minutes (the whole disc). The location of each track on a given disc in terms of absolute time in minutes and seconds relative to the start of the program area of the disc, as well as the running time of each track, is defined in the Q sub-channel in the lead-in area. The P sub-channel carries a music flag for quick track finding using a simple decoder.

The Compact Disc-Digital Audio Specification, also known as the Red Book, is available to paid-up licensees. This specification contains full details of the CD-DA system. See also CD mastering, Cross-Interleaved Reed-Solomon Code, Eight-to-Fourteen Modulation, Pulse Code Modulation.

Compact Disc drive Device specifically designed to read digital data from CD-ROM or CD-I discs. CD-I drives can also play CD-DA discs.

Compact Disc file manager A software module which handles I/O requests for the compact disc drive. Provides random access to files at the byte level through system calls.

Compact Disc-Interactive The Compact Disc-Interactive standard specifies a multi-media, interactive information carrier that is mainly real-time audio- and video-driven, but also has text, binary data and computer program capabilities. It is both a media and a system specification, and defines what can be present on the disc, how it is coded and organized, and how disc/system compatibility can be maintained.

Multi-application-based CD-I is targeted at the consumer electronic and institutional markets. It aims at satisfying a wide range of application demands for both these markets.

From a technical point of view, CD-I is based on CD-ROM, but from a player/product point of view it is based on CD-DA. Like CD-DA, it is dependent on processor hardware, but unlike CD-DA or CD-ROM, it is also system-software dependent. The reasons for CD-I's hardware and system-software dependence are motivated by, and based on, the real-time audio/video decoding and data-handling requirements that CD-I applications demand, as well as the requirement to maintain disc/system interchangeability in the same way that CD-DA does. In practical terms, this means that any CD-I disc will be able to be played on any player, regardless of where in the world both were purchased. This latter point is achieved in the CD-I specification by defining a set of rules for a minimum level system called the Base Case, which must be observed by all discs.

The CD-I specification also allows for mixing of CD-DA and CD-I tracks on CD-I discs, and requires CD-DA decoding hardware in CD-I systems.

The CD-I specification is a complete standard that: (1)is applicable to the consumer market; (2) can be realized as a one-disc, interactive, multi-media content carrier (i.e. a CD-I disc) by various content providers (e.g. publishers, the audio-visual industry etc.); (3) is capable of being produced by the existing CD manufacturing facilities; (4) assures disc/system compatibility and is, for this reason, resistant to system variations.

Satisfying all these customer requirements, and in so doing giving still higher performance levels for selected application areas, forms the basis for CD-I as an interactive multi-media carrier.

Present and potential future CD-I applicatons can be categorized as follows:

- Education and training
  - do-it-yourself
  - home learning
  - interactive training
  - reference books
  - albums
  - 'talking books'

- Entertainment
  - 'music plus' (music with text, notes, pictures etc.)
  - action games
  - adventure games
  - activity simulation
  - 'edutainment'

- Creative leisure
  - drawing/painting
  - filming
  - composing

- Work at home/while travelling
  - document processing
  - information retrieval and analysis

- While moving (e.g. in the car)
    - maps
    - navigation
    - tourist information
    - real-time animation
    - diagnostics

Compact Disc player Device specifically designed to read CD-DA discs. If provided with digital output and control interface, can also be used, in conjunction with a suitable signal processor, to read CD-ROM or CD-I discs.

Compact Disc-Read-Only Memory A natural derivative of Compact Disc-Digital Audio. Defined by Philips and Sony in 1985, the CD-ROM makes use of the identical physical characteristics - disc size, rotational speed and read-out mechanism, as well as the same disc mastering and replication processes as used for CD-Digital Audio.
Where CD-ROM and CD-DA differ is in their application. Instead of a single, dedicated application namely hi fi music, the CD-ROM specification limits itself to defining the method by which data is stored on the disc, and no more. The nature of the data, and the purpose for which it is to be interpreted, is left to the information providers making use of the medium. The disc can be divided into tracks in the same manner as for CD-DA; indeed the specification foresees the possibility of combining CD-DA tracks with CD-ROM tracks on a single disc.

CD-ROM makes use of the same CIRC error protection used in CD-DA as well as EFM (Eight-to-Fourteen Modulation). However, the data recorded on the disc is organized into sectors of 2352 bytes. Each sector is further subdivided. After 12 bytes of synchronization, and a 4-byte header to identify the address and nature, or mode, of the data in the block, the main User Data area follows, containing 2048 bytes of data. Following this area is a 288 byte long Auxiliary Data Area.
Concerning the mode information, CD-ROM normally only uses mode 1, where an additional level of error protection (EDC/ECC) is included in the Auxiliary Data Area to reduce the chance of error to less than a single bit per disc. Mode 2, also defined for CD-ROM, allocates the space used in mode 1 for error correction for recording additional user data. Mode 0 is used for CD-DA applications. The mode being used is fixed for the duration of a track. Details of the modes of all tracks are also held in the Q sub-channel in the lead-in area of each disc.
The data rate from the disc is 175 kilobytes per second. This means $175/2.352 = 75$ sectors per second. The minimum length of each track is 4 seconds, and a track contains a minimum of 300 sectors, each sector containing one 2048 byte block of user data in mode 1 and one 2336 byte

block of user data in mode 2. The total disc can contain 72 minutes of data, or in mode 1, (72 minutes) x (60 seconds) x (75 sectors) x (1 block) x (2048 bytes) = 663.5 megabytes of user information. This increases to 756.8 megabytes for mode 2. A typical type A4 page contains some 4000 bytes. Thus a CD-ROM mode 1 disc could contain over 165,000 pages of typed text. Of course this does not allow room for the necessary indexes to enable the data to be searched.

There is a selection of CD-ROM drives on the market. A series of standard hardware interfaces are also available to connect CD-ROM drives to personal computers.
CD-ROM is finding a well-defined place in the professional world for the distribution of bulk databases. Typical applications replace text based microfiche publishing, or on-line databases. In order to locate data on such a large-capacity disc as CD-ROM, personal computer versions of mainframe database retrieval software are normally used. Such software, adapted to the requirements of CD-ROM drives, used in conjunction with inverted files to identify the specific occurrence of each given word in the total database, can be used very effectively. Typical seek times of 3 to 10 seconds are now quite normal for text-based data bases of several hundred megabytes.

A further feature of CD-ROM is that the data is stored in digital form, and as such data retrieved from the disc can be reprocessed or re-edited by suitable word-processing software.
During 1985 and 1986 an ad-hoc group of CD-ROM information providers and other related companies met to attempt to extend the basic CD-ROM specification to cover such matters as file structure, file directory index, and operating system. This group, known as the High Sierra Group after the hotel in Lake Tahoe where the group first met, has now completed its study, and recommendations have been passed to the appropriate standards committees (NISO and ECMA). While Philips and Sony as owners of the basic CD-ROM standard remained aware of the work of the High Sierra Group, and indeed provided comments and suggestions to the group, no attempt was made to update the basic specification with this additional input from the High Sierra Group.

Compact Disc-Real-time Operating System CD-RTOS, the operating system used in CD-I, is specified so that the real-time capabilities of CD-I are usable, as far as possible, in a device-independent way. The features of CD-RTOS are that it:

- is a multi-tasking operating system with real-time response, has a versatile modular design, and can be loaded into ROM.

- supports a variety of arithmetic and I/O co-processors

- is device-independent and interrupt-driven
- can handle multi-level tree-structured disc directories
- supports both byte-addressable random-access files and real- time files and
- is OS-9 compatible.

CD-RTOS is composed of four major blocks:

- Libraries; these guarantee that the necessary specialized user library functions such as high-level access and data synchronization, as well as math, I/O and other functions are available in CD-I systems. One of the most important of these is synchronization.
- CD-RTOS kernel; this is a customized version of the OS-9 kernel.
- Managers; these define the virtual device level for graphics, visuals, text, audio, CD control etc. The managers provide software support for graphics/visual devices, pointing devices, and the CD-I audio processing devices, as well as taking care of disc I/O and optimized disc access and reading.
- Drivers; these are the interfaces between the virtual, i.e. hardware-independent, level and the actual hardware used by various manufacturers in their CD-I systems.

compatibility In Compact Disc, the extent to which different types of discs can be interpreted by different types of players or drives. For example, all CD-DA discs are fully compatible with all CD-DA players, so that any player can reproduce music from any disc regardless of manufacturer.

compression A technique in which the amount of information used to present a specific image is reduced by eliminating redundant or unnecessary information.

computer graphics Pictures created by computer programs. Standard drawing functions such as 'line', 'circle', etc. are normally used.

concealment In digital signal processing, the hiding of errors e.g. by an interpolation scheme.

concurrent (audio) channel Block multiplexed audio information. CD-I allows for up to 16 audio channnels to be recorded concurrently on the disc, so that by playing the disc several times and accessing different channels, extended playing time is obtained or by playing the disc once, the same or related audio information may be obtained from parallel channels, e.g. the same information in a different language.

configuration status descriptor Describes the configuration of a particular CD-I system. Composed of device status descriptors.

constant angular velocity A disc rotation mode in which the disc always rotates at the same speed, so that the time of one revolution is always the same.

constant linear velocity A disc rotation mode in which the discrotation speed changes as the read radius changes so that the linear reading speed i.e. the speed at which the read-out device scans the track, is always the same. Maximizes disc information storage capacity.

content provider In CD-I, the writer, publisher or other party(ies) supplying information, usually copyrighted, for an application.

CRC See cyclic redundancy check.

Cross-Interleaved Reed-Solomon Code (CIRC) An error protection code specially developed for Compact Disc. It consists of two Reed-Solomon codes interleaved crosswise.

CIRC makes it possible for a CD player decoder to detect and correct or conceal large burst errors. Errors up to 4000 data bits (2.5 mm of track) can be corrected. Errors up to 12,304 data bits can be concealed.
The CIRC encoder uses 2 stages of encoding and 3 stages of interleaving. The 12 PCM audio samples (24 symbols) of one Compact Disc audio frame are fed in parallel to the first encoder. The second symbol of each audio sample is delayed by two symbols, so that the symbols of two successive frames are interleaved. The first encoder then adds 4 parity symbols, making 28 in all.
These 28 symbols are fed to the second encoder through delay lines of different lengths. The second encoder adds four more parity symbols, making 32 in all. Finally, alternative audio signals are delayed by one symbol. The total effect is to spread the symbols of one frame over eight frames.

The two stages of CIRC encoding make it possible for the CIRC decoder in a CD player to correct two symbols in each received frame directly, or to correct four symbols in each received frame by erasure and calculation. Furthermore, it allows detection of up to 32 successive incorrect symbols so that interpolated values can be substituted. Because of the dispersion of symbols over 8 frames, up to 4000 wrong data bits can be corrected and up to 12,304 wrong data bits can be concealed. The final (1 symbol) delay provides protection against random errors. See also Compact Disc-Digital Audio, eight-to-fourteen modulation.

CSD see configuration status descriptor

cue code In Compact Disc, a code used in tape mastering. Recorded on audio track 1 of the CD-tape master, it contains the information necessary to generate subcode during disc mastering. See CD mastering.

cursor plane A small graphical image plane that can be moved around the display or made invisible as required. It can be positioned at any position over the other planes.

cut A basic effect in film and video editing which causes an image to appear, usually to replace a previous image.

cut and paste An electronic technique for the manipulation of textual or pictorial information on a display screen in a manner similar to the cut and paste technique used in editing such information on paper.

CVBS Composite video broadcast signal. The standard form of color TV broadcast signal in which the intensity and relation of the red, green and blue components are represented by a luminance signal and a chrominance signal.

cyclic redundancy check In Compact Disc, a separate error detection scheme for the Compact Disc subcode.

DAT See Digital Audio Tape.

data channel (1) In CD, a channel carrying data, as opposed to audio information. (2) In CD-ROM, a channel carrying mode 1 data.

data driven action tagging In CD-I, the technique for identifying or tagging events on the different data streams (audio, video, text/data) so that they can be synchronized according to the requirements of the application program.

data integrity The preservation, against loss or corruption, of programs or data for their intended purposes.

data symbol An entity made up of n bits representing a value between ·0 and 2^{n-1}.

data track A track with information encoded as 8-bit wide symbols (bytes) organized in sectors.

delta modulation In data communications, a form of differential PCM in which only 1 bit for each sample is used.

delta pulse code modulation See delta modulation.

delta-YUV A high-efficiency image-coding scheme for natural pictures used in CD-I. The delta coding takes advantage of the fact that there is a high correlation between adjacent pixel values, making it possible to encode only the differences between the absolute YU or YV pixel values. This coding scheme is applied per line i.e. in one dimension. See YUV encoding.

differential PCM In data communications, a version of pulse code modulation in which the difference in value between a sample and the previous sample is encoded. Fewer bits are thus required for transmission than under PCM. In CD-I, this technique is applied in video encoding as well as audio encoding. See adaptive delta pulse code modulation, delta YUV.

digital audio tape Internationally agreed standard for digital audio tape recording. Digital Audio Tape cassettes, although noticeably smaller than Compact Cassettes, can record up to 2 hours of continuous digital quality sound. Recordings are made diagonally on tape by a twin rotary recording head. In a similar way to CD-DA discs, digital audio tape recordings incorporate CIRC error protection for high sound quality and long life. They also include a control and display subcode for highly convenient playback.

digital magnetic tape Magnetic tape with a thin base layer for precision tape-head contact, and a high linear density (approximately 20 times that of analog tape) to accommodate the bit packing requirement of 20 kbits per inch.

digital recording Recording audio or video signals in digital form. The level of the signal to be recorded is sampled at a rate at least double the highest frequency to be reproduced, and the instantaneous amplitude of the signal is quantized and stored in numerical or digital form.

direct RGB coding Picture coding scheme used in CD-I for high-quality (e.g. modelled) graphics that can easily be changed by the user. Images are encoded on disc as red, green and blue components using 5 bits for each color plus one overlay or control bit.

directly addressable sector A sector that may be addressed directly in terms of time and number of sectors from a given reference point - normally the start of the first data track on the disc.

directory record A record describing one file in a directory.

directory search method The method used to locate a specific file on the disc. This method allows any file to be opened using only one seek.

disc bootstrap routine Optional routine on a CD-I disc to add or replace operating system capabilities in a Base Case system.

disc interchangeability The ability to exchange discs between players of different manufacture. This is an essential feature of both CD-DA and CD-I.

disc file protection mechanism A method of allowing multiple products to reside on a single CD-I disc and forcing the consumer to purchase each product before it can be used.

disc label The information in the first track of a disc concerning the disc type and format, the status of the disc as a single entity or part of an album, the data size and the position of the file directory and boot modules.

disc map The organization of data on magnetic tape as it will be on the CD disc.

disc replication The production of copy discs from a master disc, usually for commercial distribution.

disc storage Data storage on optical or magnetic disc, characterised by low cost and relatively fast data access, compared with tape storage.

disc/system validation The procedure for checking the correct operation of a CD-I disc or a CD-I system using a 'reference' CD-I system or 'reference' CD-I disc respectively.

display (1) Generally, a device for presentation of visual information which varies with time. (2) The visual image on the screen of a display unit or monitor.

display controller Two-path device which takes pixel data from the two banks of RAM of a CD-I player and combines them to produce a single analog RGB video output.

display control program (DCP)   A set of command codes are interpreted by the display hardware during either the horizontal or vertical retrace periods. The codes can be used to perform a variety of functions; background colors, entries for color look- up tables, display parameters, etc.

display resolution The measure of the number of pixels, and thus the amount of detail, that a screen can display.

display unit Synonymous with video display.

dissolve The simultaneous fade-up of one image and fade-down of a second image.

double-frequency scanning A method of scanning at twice the normal frequency so that double the number of lines can be shown within one frame, without the loss of quality or the line flicker of normal interlaced scanning. Improves the vertical resolution of the display.

double resolution   Twice as many pixels as a normal resolution image in the horizontal direction, but the same number in the vertical direction.

double word A numeric entity comprising twice the number of bits contained in a normal computer word. For a 16-bit processor the double word is 32 bits wide; for a 32-bit processor it is 64 bits wide. Occupies two successive memory locations.

DPCM See delta modulation.

drawmap   A block of memory allocated by the User Communications Manager to store image data.

driver Distinguishes hardware-specific features of CD-I players and implements functions of file managers and isolates software for hardware functions.

dynamic loading In CD-I, updating the contents of the color look-up table (CLUT) during the horizontal retrace period (up to 4 colors) or during the vertical retrace period (up to 256 colors).

DYUV See delta YUV

ECC See error correction code.

EDC See error detection code.

EFM See eight-to-fourteen modulation.

eight-to-fourteen modulation In Compact Disc, the pulse code modulated signal produced by analog-to-digital conversion is a simple non-return-to-zero bit stream of 1s and 0s. It is not self-clocking, and there is no restriction on Run-Length. (The number of successive 1s and 0s). To record this signal directly on to the disc would not only be inefficient in terms of disc storage capacity. It would also make playback very difficult, if not impossible.

Eight-to-Fourteen Modulation (EFM) is therefore applied, to produce a signal format suitable for recording. EFM imposes a minimum Run-Length of 3 bits and a maximum Run-Length of 11 bits. It also changes the signal into a non-return-to-zero inverted bit stream, in which a 1 is represented by a transition, and a 0 by no transition. Finally, EFM introduces a unique synchronization pattern to each frame of audio information.

EFM greatly reduces the number of transitions for the same amount of data. This means that the data can be read more reliably, with much less risk of interference between symbols. It also means that 25% more data can be recorded on the same disc area. At the same time, EFM ensures that there are always enough transitions to allow bit clock regeneration in the Compact Disc player. The data is thus made self-clocking.

EFM also minimizes the difference between the number of 1s and the number of 0s in the bit stream. This suppresses low frequency components which could otherwise interfere with the player's focussing, tracking and motor control servos.

Finally, the synchronization pattern allows each frame to be recognized. This is essential, particularly for error correction and subcode separation. EFM changes each 8-bit symbol in the signal into a 14-bit symbol. The 14-bit symbols all have a minimum of 3 and a maximum of 11 successive 0s. 256 such symbols are needed to match all the possible 8-bit combinations. (In fact 267 14-bit symbols meet this requirement; 11 are not used). The 256 14-bit symbols form a look-up table held in a RAM. The Run-Length conditions must be maintained between symbols as well as within them. This is achieved by inserting two merging bits. A third merging bit maintains the balance between the number of 1s and 0s in the bit stream.

Thus, each 8-bit symbol becomes a 17-bit symbol (14 +3). The synchronization pattern consists of 24 bits, and is uniquely identifiable. It, too, has 3 merging bits.

An eight-to-fourteen modulated audio frame is composed of 33 seventeen-bit symbols (24 audio, 8 parity and 1 subcode) plus a 27-bit synchronization pattern; a total of 588 'channel bits'. This is the signal written on to the disc, where each 1 is represented by the beginning or end of a pit. See also Compact Disc-Digital Audio, pulse code modulation.

electronic publishing   A generic term for the distribution of information on computer databases linked by communication networks. Videotex is an example of this method of publishing.

electronic storyboard An electronic version of a storyboard, usually in the form of computer software program, used in the development of among other things, a CD-I disc design.

end-of-file bit A bit in the submode byte of the subheader that is set to 1 for the last sector of a real-time file

end-of-record bit A bit in the submode byte of the subheader that is set to 1 for the last sector of a real-time record.

EOF-bit See end-of-file bit

EOR-bit See end-of-record bit

erasable optical disc Research into erasable media suitable for use in optical discs has been under way for some time at Philips Research Laboratories and elsewhere. Two main technologies have so far emerged. The first of these uses a technique known as magneto-optical recording, and erasable optical discs have been produced experimentally. Writing and reading depend on the physical effects of small, reverse-polarised magnetic domains in a thin polarized magnetic layer. Writing is performed by reversing the polarization of the domain, while under the influence of an external magnetic field, by heating it above the compensation point temperature with a short laser pulse. Reading is performed by measuring the Kerr effect, which rotates polarized light when it is reflected under the influence of a magnetic field.

The second method under investigation uses the inherant difference in reflectivity of the crystalline form and non- crystalline (amorphous) form of the same material as a starting point. The information is recorded by rapidly heating small areas in a thin layer of crystalline material to slightly above its melting point with a fairly powerful laser beam. These small areas then solidify (the 'supercooled phase'). This produces amorphous areas in a crystalline material and these can be detected optically by the variation in reflectance. The differences in reflectivity are quite sufficient for digital readout and sufficiently well defined for the reproduction of analog video signals.

Because the crystalline form of materials is the most stable, all materials tend to change into this phase. This effect can be used to erase information on the disc. Heating to just below the melting point with a laser beam will return the material to its fully crystalline state.

As a result of research work into amorphous-crystallinematerials, gallium antimonide and indium antimonide were discovered as suitable materials during the course of 1986.

These materials have a long shelf life, and are insensitive to ordinary ambient temperatures and to humidity. Information can be erased and re-recorded about a thousand times, which is quite sufficient for consumer applications.

Research into these possibilities for erasable optical recording continues. Improvements in the signal-to-noise ratio can be expected, as well as the number of times that information can be erased and rerecorded.

error concealment A variety of techniques used in concealing errors in visual images displayed from a CD-I disc.

error correction Identification and correction of errors arising in the transfer of information. Used extensively in computer storage media such as Compact Discs. See Cross-Interleaved Reed-Solomon Code, cyclic redundancy check, error correction code, error detection code.

error correction code (1) In computing and communications, a code designed to detect an error, in a word or character, identify the incorrect bit and replace it with the correct one. (2) An error correction code used in CD-ROM and CD-I to achieve high data integrity. See form 1, mode 1.

error detection code (1) In computing and communications, a code designed to detect, but not correct, an error in a word or character. (2) An error detection code used in CD-ROM and CD-I to achieve high data integrity. See form 1, mode 1.

executable code A set of instructions, or a computer program, in the machine language for a specific computer or microprocesor, and which can be executed, or run, directly.

executable object code The output from a compiler's or assembler's linkage editor or linker, which is in the machine code for a particular processor, with each loadable program being one named file (module). In CD-I, such an object file does not contain audio or video data. See executable code.

extended disc In CD-I, a hypothetical disc that can exercise all the capabilities of an 'extended' system as defined by the CD-I 'extended' system specification. The Base Case specification is a subset of the 'extended' system specification.

extended system In CD-I, a system conforming to Base Case specification, plus any extensions that conform to the 'extended' CD-I system specification.

extension (1) In CD-I, an upward compatible module to replace an existing system module in ROM. During initialization, all modules in CD-RTOS (except the protection modules) may be replaced by extended modules which have revision numbers higher than the ones they replace. (2) In CD-I, a hardware module supporting a functional extension conforming to the CD-I 'extended' system specification. During initialization, CD-RTOS identifies the extension and includes the software modules from it.

fade A gradual decrease (fade-out) or increase (fade-in) of the brightness of an image, or the volume of an audio signal.

field control table A one-dimensional array of instructions which are carried out before the start of each field.

file A collection of logically related records identifyable in a directory.

file descriptor record A sector found in all CD-I files, containing a list of the data segments, their starting logical sector number, size and file attributes. Needed to access files on a disc.

file manager In CD-I, a system software module which handles I/O requests for the CD drive. Provides random access to files at the byte level through system calls.

file structure volume descriptor Record of the Disc Label describing all necessary items related to the files or parts of the files recorded on the volume.

file protection A mechanism whereby access to information in a given file is resticted to those possessing the valid access key.

flowchart A chart indicating the interactive and pseudo-linear structure of the disc.

form bit Bit in the submode byte of the subheader field defining the data form (Form 1 or Form 2) for the sector.

form 1 The CD-I sector format with EDC/ECC error detection and correction. Equivalent to CD-ROM mode 1, but with the form identity included in a sub-header to permit interleaving of form 1 and form 2 sectors to meet the requirements of real-time operation.

form 2 The CD-I sector format with an auxiliary data field instead of EDC/ECC error detection and correction. Equivalent to CD-ROM mode 2, but with the form identity included in a sub-header to permit interleaving of form 1 and form 2 sectors to meet the requirements of real-time operation.

frame (1) In computing the array of bits across the width of magnetic or paper tape. (2) An individual picture on a film, filmstrip or videotape. (3) A single television tube picture scan combining interlaced information. (4) In videotex, a page of data displayed on a terminal. (5) In CD-DA, one complete pattern of digital audio information, comprising 6 PCM stereo samples, with CIRC and one subcode symbol, eight-to-fourteen modulated, with a synchronization pattern.

frame grabber (1) In recording, an electronic technique for storing and regenerating a video frame from a helical video tape signal. This method avoids the need for the continuous head to tape contact that would otherwise be required in freeze frame operation. (2) An electronic device for extracting a complete frame from a video signal and storing it in memory for further processing.

full-motion video Not a design option in full screen for CD-I at this time. However, a combination of the video bit set to 1, form bit set to 0 and real-time sector bit set to 1 is reserved for full-screen full-motion video.

genlock A capability planned for CDI-X in which the background plane will be synchronized to an external video source, allowing the CD-I application to interact with external video information.

glass master An optical master disc produced by exposing a photosensitive coating on a glass substrate to a laser beam, then developing the exposed coating and covering it with a silver coating. See CD-disc master, CD mastering.

global dissolve A dissolve affecting the whole of a video picture. Compare local dissolve.

global fade A fade affecting the whole of a video picture. Compare local fade.

global search A search operation performed on a complete file or database. Compare local search.

glyph The bitmap image for a symbol. For example, the bitmap image of the letter "a" is the glyph for the letter "a".

graceful degradation In CD-I, degradation of audio or video quality due to increasing error content.

granulation An effect whereby the resolution of an image changes without its size altering. It is produced by a combination of pixel hold and line hold functions.

graphics cursor functions User Communications Manager functions which control the shape, size, color and position of the graphics cursor on the display screen.

graphics drawing functions User Communications Manager functions which are used to draw images in drawmaps.

group execute (file attribute bit) This bit of the attribute field of a directory record specifies that only users belonging to an identified group can execute the program contained in this file.

group read (file attribute bit) This bit of the attribute field of a directory record specifies that only users belonging to an identified group can access this file.

green book Informal name for the CD-I specification.

hardware-dependent Of a system, dependent for its operation on a specific hardware configuration.

header field In CD-ROM or CD-I, the second level of audio quality. A bandwidth of 17000 Hz is obtained using 8-bit ADPCM at a sampling frequency of 37.8 MHz. Comparable with LP record sound quality. See audio quality level.

high resolution (1) The degree of detailed visual definition (800 x 600 pixels) that gives readable 80 column text display. (2) In CD-I, a display resolution mode of 768 pixels (horizontal) by 560 pixels (vertical). Compare normal resolution, double resolution.

High Sierra group An ad-hoc standards group set up to recommend compatible standards for CD-ROM. The group includes representatives from the hardware, software and publishing industries, and was named after the hotel in Lake Tahoe where it first met in the summer of 1985.

horizontal line update The modification of all or part of a single line in a video image.

horizontal retrace period Time during which the horizontal line scan on a TV screen returns to the beginning of the next line.

hot spots Synonymous with active areas.

hyper-media An extension of hyper-text incorporating cross-linked databases contained not only data in the form of text, but also in the form of music, voice, sound effects, graphics, as well as still and moving visuals.

hyper-text A series of logically interlinked databases, where the information within one database can be logically cross-linked with the related information in another.

icon Pictorial representation of an object in a graphic display.

idea map An overview of a CD-I disc project in the form of a map-like structure, charting the relationships between individual elements making up the disc content, in such a way that the links between previously undefined elements can be established with a degree of confidence.

ideogram Symbol or character conveying an idea, expression or part thereof (e.g. a Kanji character).

image A full or reduced screen image, or a partial update or an irregular partial update.

image plane A displayed image may be formed by the superimposition of a number of component pictures. Each of these constitutes an image The CD-I system has a maximum of four image planes including the cursor and backdrop planes.

information area Synonymous with recorded area.

information exchange protocol (IXP) A protocol for labelling and describing data on a CD-I disc which is used in the mastering process. This data describes the media type and encoding techniques, among other characteristics. This data may also include other descriptions of the disc data which might be useful to the mastering facility.

information carrier Any medium by which information is carried from its point of origin to its point of use, e.g. magnetic tape,Compact Disc, transmission line, broadcasting channel, or paper.

input port An interface used for transferring information into a computer. See I/O port.

insert module A module which, when inserted into an equipment or system, enables it to perform additional functions.

intelligent player A CD player with additional computing facilities built in, enabling the player to interact with the user, or to operate under program control. CD-I players are intelligent players.

interactive LaserVision A system which employs a LaserVision drive and a (micro)computer, either built-in or external, to run interactive programs from a CAV type LaserVision disc.

interactive medium Medium which presents information in such a way that, by means of an application program, it is delivered in the course of a dialog with the user. The application program may also be included in the medium. Examples include Interactive LaserVision and CD-I.

interactive mode Presentation of information in a sequence determined by a dialog between the information medium and the recipient. Compare linear mode. See interactive medium.

interactive system A system capable of using an interactive medium to supply information to the user.

interactive video (IV) Synonymous with interactive LaserVision.

interlace A system of picture scanning using two fields, the lines of the second field being interposed between those of the first. Interlace scanning produces a higher level of detail while minimizing the flicker inherent with low refresh rates.

interleaving In CD-I, the process of physically separating data so it can be retrieved at the rate required for processing the data. It involves the interspacing of sectors at intervals that correspond to the nature of the data. For audio, a regular interspaced pattern is used which depends on the audio quality level required. The subheader indicates the interleaving pattern at file, channel and data type levels. Blocks between consecutive audio blocks can be used for video or text data.

International Standard Recording Code A code used by record manufacturers. Gives information about country of origin, owner, year of issue and serial number of individual music tracks. May optionally appear in CD-DA subcode.

interpolation scheme A method of concealing errors.

InVision A user interface toolkit developed by Microware. Most CD-I players will have InVision in ROM.

I/O functions In CD-I, the transfer functions Read and Play which perform the physical transfer of data from the disc.

I/O port An opening on a CD-I player or microcomputer enabling an external device to be connected for input/output operation.

irregular updates One of the two types of partial updates available within CD-I, where the area to be updated is irregular in shape.

ISRC See International Standard Recording Code.

ISO 646 International Standard specifying the 7-bit coded character set for information interchange.

ISO 2022 International Standard specifying the methods (through shift function or escape sequences) to extend 7 or 8 bit coded character sets.

ISO 2375 International Standard specifying the registration procedure of escape sequences used for code extension of a character set. It refers particularly to the International Register of coded character sets to be used with escape sequences.

ISO 8859/1 The specification of the coded character set for Latin alphabet No. 1 used as the standard character set definition for CD-I machines.

IV Interactive Video. Synonymous with interactive LaserVision.

IXP Information exchange protocol.

kernel The nucleus of CD-RTOS.

keyboard input functions User Communications manager functions which are used to get character data from a keyboard device.

LaserVision Optical video disc system developed by Philips for reproducing and 2-channel sound.

lead-in area In CD, a track (number 0) on the disc preceding the program areas. Contains the table of contents.

lead-out area In CD, a track (number $AA) on the disc following the program area.

line control table A two-dimensional array of instructions, each row of which is associated with the displayed line.

line hold, line repeat In the vertical direction, mosaic graphics are produced by holding and repeating lines.

line multiplication A technique used in CD-I to make high-resolution line information compatible with a lower-resolution system.

linear mode Presentation of information in a fixed sequence, un-influenced by the recipient. Compare interactive mode.

line update The modification of single line, or part of a line, of graphics stored on a file.

linker See linking loader.

load time In video, the time taken to put a complete picture on the screen.

loadable program A single named file containing object code information used in CD-I.

local dissolve A dissolve affecting a portion of the image. Compare global dissolve.

local fade A fade affecting a portion of an image. Compare global fade.

local search A search operation confined to part of a file or database. Compare global search.

low resolution A degree of detailed visual definition below the 400 x 300 pixels presented by normal domestic color TV sets. Compare normal resolution, double resolution, high resolution.

luminance The measured radiance of a light source expressed by Y signals. Compare chrominance.

LV See LaserVision.

master disc An original disc, from which copies can be made by a replication process. See CD Disc master.

mastering In optical disc, the production of the master disc.

main channel address The address in time, seconds and sector numbers on the main channel of a given sector.

matte An area on an image plane which is made transparent, permitting the image behind it to show through. A matte can also be defined so that the area itself remains visible, while everything around becomes transparent.

media palette In CD-I, the available range of technology functions for storing information on a CD-I disc, for use in a range of specific design applications.

memory module A named block of executable program statements or data that can be loaded by CD-RTOS into memory.

metal father A recording mould formed by nickel plating on a master disc. Can be used directly for replication, or as the basis for the production, by two further stages of plating, of stampers for large-quantity production.

menu-driven The course of events in an application program, interactively controlled by means of menu selections.

message sector Sector containing caution encoded as CD-DA audio data to warn the user of a CD-DA player to lower the volume.

mid fi quality In CD-I, the third level of audio quality. A bandwidth of 12000 Hz is obtained by using 4-bit ADPCM at a sampling rate of 37.7 kHz. Comparable with FM broadcast sound quality. See audio quality level.

mix The combination of two (or more) images into a single image.

mode 1 One of the two physical sector formats defined for CD-ROM. Incorporates EDC/ECC error detection and correction.

mode 2 One of the two physical formats defined for CD-ROM. Incorporates an auxiliary data field instead of EDC/ECC error detection and correction.

mode byte In CD-ROM, the byte in the header field of a sector that defines whether a sector is mode 1, mode 2 or mode FF.

mode FF IXP information

mosaic graphics In CD-I, low-resolution graphics achieved by repeating pixels or lines by a certain factor.

mother In disc replication, a negative mould intermediate between metal father and stamper. Formed by nickel plating on the metal father. See metal father.

multiplane A video image in which various different pictures are overlaid one on top of the other.

natural images Pictures which are photographic in nature and appear realistic.

natural pictures See natural images.

near-instantaneous compression Compression performed quickly enough to have no perceptible effect on the timing of the presentation of the information concerned.

new media Media now becoming available, or envisaged as becoming available, for mass information presentation.

non-linear quantization Quantization using steps of different sizes, to distribute the steps more efficiently over the dynamic range. Takes advantage of the fact that quantization errors are less perceptible when signal changes are large.

non volatile random access memory Memory able to retain its contents when the main power to the unit is removed.

normal resolution In CD-I, a display resolution mode of 384 horizontal pixels by 280 vertical pixels. The lowest resolution picture defined in the CD-I system. Compare low resolution, high resolution, double resolution.

NV-RAM Non volatile random access memory.

omni player A CD-Video player that will play CD-I discs.

object code The code of a user's program after it has been translated by means of an assembler or a compiler.

odd/even line separation When error concealment is to be used, the even and odd lines of an image are coded on a disc in separate sectors and are physically separated by interleaving so as to minimize the chance of an error occuring on adjacent lines.

on-board Additional or supporting function incorporated into a printed-circuit board or within the housing of an equipment.

one dimensional Run-Length coding A picture coding technique in which pixel data is compressed using Run-Length coding in the horizontal direction only.

optical digital disc An optical disc in which information is stored digitally.

optical disc A disc in which information is impressed as a series of pits in a flat surface, and is read out by optical means, i.e. by a laser.

optical input In optical media, the light signal before it is converted into an electrical signal.

optical medium Medium employing optics for the storage and distribution of information.

optical recording The recording of information in such a way that it can be read by a beam of light. Modern optical recording technology is almost entirely concentrated on the use of low-power lasers to write and read information on optical discs. Optical discs can carry very large amounts of information per unit volume. They are highly resistant to damage and immune to electromagnetic influences. Access to information is fast and error rates can be made very low. Laser read-out completely eliminates wear during use.

DOR Digital Optical Recording systems can write and read digital data (though at present without any erasure facility). Their principal application is in large-scale archiving.

Rapid developments are being made in read-only optical recording systems, which include CD-DA, CD-ROM and CD-I.

optical storage Storage of information in such a way that it can be read using optics. Characterised by very high storage density.

optical technology Technology based on the use of optical effects for the transmission or storage of information.

OS-9 The real-time operating system which forms the basis for the CD-I operating system CD-RTOS.

output port An interface used for transferring information out of a computer. See I/O port.

overlay The process of superimposing image planes in a given visual image.

overlay control In CD-I, the mechanism which controls transparency between planes.

overscan Extending the deflection of the electron beam of a cathode ray tube (CRT) is made to extend beyond the usable physical dimensions of the screen. In this way images will always fill the visible part of the display screen.

owner execute (file attribute bit) This bit of the attribute field of a directory record if set to one specifies that only the user identified as "owner" of the file can execute the program contained in this file.

owner read (file attribute bit) This bit of the attribute field of a directory record specifies that only the user identified as "owner" of the file can access this file.

palette A range of colors. In CD-I, a palette is used by the User Communications Manager to support the color look-up table. The maximum size of the palette at any instant in time is 256 colors, with the red, green and blue components each defined to 8-bit accuracy. See media palette.

panning The distribution of a mono signal between left and right audio channels.

parent directory A directory which contains sub-directories.

partial update New image data written to part of a picture that is currently being displayed.

path descriptor A data structure used to represent an open file; each open file is associated with a path descriptor.

path table Table or index used for directory search. Describes an entire directory structure on a disc. Permits any file on the disc to be opened using only one search.

P channel One of the eight Compact Disc subcode channels (P-W). The P channel carries the music flag, indicating presence of absence of a music track.

PCM See pulse code modulation.

PCM audio (1) A pulse-code-modulated audio signal. (2) In CD-DA the audio signal after the first stage of encoding i.e. a multiplexed signal with six 32-bit stereo samples in each audio frame.

photosensor Any device for converting light into an electrical signal.

picture element Synonymous with pixel.

Pixel The smallest element on an image which can be manipulated or identified. Synonymous with picture element.

pixel aspect ratio The ratio of width to height of a displayed pixel. Ideally this should be 1:1.

pixel hold Method used to reduce resolution. This function operates after the pixel codes have been decoded to RGB.

pixel pairing Pixel pairing occurs in 3-bit run-coded images and 4-bit CLUT encoded pictures. Two pixels are put together to make up one byte, and are then regarded for most purposes (e.g. the length of the run in run-coded pictures) as a single unit.

pixel repeat A visual effect function that repeats pixel values from an image memory to produce horizontal magnification. Used in RGB 5:5:5 and CLUT image decoding.

plane See image plane.

play control block A data structure indicating what information is to be accessed on the disc for the current or next real-time record play function of the compact disc file manager.

play control list A structure list that controls the destination of the data.

players default character set Set of characters selected by the current user of the player when a disc is initially accessed. For CD-I this conforms to ISO/DIS 8859/1.

prediction filters The filters used in ADPCM encoding to achieve effective response to audio frequency distribution fluctuations.

pre-mastering The stage between authoring and mastering.

program carrier Material or device to carry or store a program.

program area The area of a Compact Disc containing the program and consisting of a maximum of 99 audio or data tracks.

program related data Data in the form of executable object code to be read and processed by the CD-I MPU.

programmable sound generator Audio signal generator with an integrated microprocessor to control the output signal according to a program set up by the user.

pulse code modulation (PCM) A technique for converting analog information into CD-DA digital form. The analog signal is sampled at a rate equal to at least twice the maximum signal frequency component, and the sampled value is represented by afixed length binary number. This number is then transmitted as a corresponding set of pulses.

Q channel One of the eight Compact Disc subcode channels (P-W). The Q channel carries the main control and display information. It identifies tracks, indexes and running times, and the absolute playing time of the disc. It also indicates whether the recorded information is audio or data, whether pre-emphasis is applied and whether digital copying is permitted. It can also indicate 2 or 4 channel audio, should 4-channel audio be introduced. Optionally, it can include a disc catalog number and ISRC information. Finally, it includes its own CRC (cyclic redundancy check).

QHY See quantized high Y.

QHY quantization levels The QHY difference values, which need to be added to the normal resolution quantities to generate a pseudo-high resolution image, are 8-bit quantities varying between 0 and 255. Eight values are chosen from these 256 possible quantities. Each difference value is then made equal to the nearest of these eight, and a three bit number is used to represent it. The eight chosen values are known as quantization levels.

quantize To assign one of a fixed set of values to an analog signal as part of an analog to digital conversion process e.g. in pulse code modulation, an analog signal is sampled, quantized and a corresponding set of binary pulses is produced. See pulse code modulation.

quantized high Y A coding technique used to reduce the quantity of data required to encode a high resolution type picture. A normal resolution DYUV image is recorded together with the data which needs to be added to it to turn the luminance (Y) of the picture to the equivalent of high resolution. The latter data further compressed is termed 'QHY'.

quantizer A device or circuit which assigns fixed binary values to sampled analog signals in analog-to-digital conversion.

quick disc Optical disc produced on very short delivery (normally during one working day) to a special requirement or for program validation prior to disc replication.

RAM Random access memory.

random access memory In computing, (1) a memory chip used with microprocessors, information can be read from, and written into, the memory but the contents are lost when the power supply is removed, (2) any form of storage in which the access time for any item of data is independent of the location of the data most recently obtained.

random area update An area of any shape, updated as a succession of horizontal whole or partial line updates.

random error In computing, a spontaneous bit error, usually not re-producible and independent of the data. This type of error is caused by device operation up to physical boundaries.

raw sector A sector of information that includes the subheader, data and error correction information.

read/write medium A medium that can be both written (record) and read (playback). Magnetic media can generally be written, read, erased and re-written repeatedly. Optical carriers are at present read-only, or write once, read many times (WORM). Erasable optical discs are the subject of intensive research.

read error An error in the reading of data from a storage medium.

real-time control area Disc sector preceding some real-time records that contains all control data and specific instructions for playback.

real-time data In CD-I, data taken directly from the disc, whose flow cannot be interrupted or stopped within the bounds of a real-time record.

real-time file A file containing at least one real-time record.

real-time interactive system An interactive system which responds to events directly as they occur, i.e. in real-time. CD-I is a real-time interactive system.

real-time operating system An operating system that functions within the constraints of real-time, e.g. CD-RTOS, the OS-9-based operating system of CD-I. Such an operating system is essential for full interactivity.

real-time record In CD-I, the smallest amount of real-time data that can be randomly accessed. A logical record in a CD-I file containing audio, video, and/or computer data that must be retrieved from a CD-I disc at a precise rate.

real-time record interpreter A trap-handler module which an application can use to assist in the playback of real-time records.

real-time sector In CD-I, a sector with the real-time bit set. The data in this sector must be processed without interrupting the real-time behaviour of the CD-I system.

record The logical component(s) of a file.

recorded area The total area of the recording on a Compact Disc including the lead-in area, the program area and the lead-out area.

rectangular update One of the two types of partial updates available within CD-I, where the area to be updated is in rectangular form.

red book Informal name for the CD - DA specification.

reduced resolution The magnification effect produced by pixel and line repeat may be used to produce a low resolution image allowing fast update from the disc of a larger than normal screen area. This is an alternative to animation, like Run-Length compression, which may be chosen for specific applications.

reduced screen display   A display consisting of the safety area surrounded by an appropriate border.

refresh rate The frequency with which new visual information can be put up on a screen.

region   A software mechanism in the User Communications Manager which is used to limit the area of drawing in a drawmap, and to set up mattes.

region generation In video, an overlay technique defining the overlay area separate from the image contents.

replication The production of copies from a master, usually for commercial distribution.

retrieval   The process of searching for, locating and reading out data.

RGB encoding A video encoding technique which transforms the red, blue and green components of a video signal into a PCM signal.

RGB (5:5:5) One of the video encoding techniques used for images in CD-I. For each pixel the colors (red, green and blue) are each quantized and represented by 5 bits of information, giving 32 levels of intensity from one extreme value to the other. See also absolute RGB components.

ROM see read-only memory

root directory The highest level directory contained on a disc. A root directory must reside on every CD-I disc.

RL See Run-Length.

RLE See Run-Length (en)coding.

rotational latency The time taken for the disc to rotate under the read head until the required block becomes available for reading.

RTCA See real-time control area.

RTOS See real-time operating system.

RTR See real-time record.

RTRI See real-time record interpreter.

Run-Length In a data stream, the number of bits between transitions.

Run-Length (en)coding A picture data compression technique which uses two-byte codes. The first byte identifies color, and the second byte tells the decoder how many pixels are to be of this color.

running time In CD-DA, the time that an audio track has been running. Included in the subcode and thus available for display during playback.

safety area That part of an image (expressed in terms of pixel coordinates) that is guaranteed to be displayed despite all tolerance values that can occur in monitors and TV sets.

sample rate converter Unit which converts the sampling rate of a digital audio signal.

SAT Stanford Achievement Test. Used by US Universities as a measure of eligibility for University entrance

scan convertor A device used in presenting a non-interlaced picture on a normal TV screen containing the same number of lines as the original interlaced picture. See also double-frequency scanning.

scrambling In CD-I, all data except for the data in the synchronization field is scrambled. The contents of a 15-bit shift register scrambler is EXOR-ed with the serial information bit by bit.

scramble register A register used in the scrambling and descrambling process for all data in a CD-I sector.

screen (1) Video display. (2) Displayed image

scroll The repeated repositioning of a displayed image within a large image. Motion may be vertical, horizontal or a combination of the two.

search program A program that searches a data file or database to find a keyword or key phrase supplied by an operator or another program. See retrieval.

sector The smallest unit of absolutely addressable information in a CD-ROM or CD-I disc. A sector is 2352 bytes long containing a synchronization pattern, header field and digital data. It may also contain a sub-header and EDC/ECC error protection. See sector structure.

sector address In CD-ROM and CD-I, the physical address of a sector expressed in minutes, seconds and sector number. Contained in the address part of the sector header.

sector structure In CD-ROM and CD-I, the 2352 sequential bytes of a sector may be divided in one of four ways, depending on the system and the degree of data integrity required. See the accompanying table.

CD-ROM and CD-I sector structure

	CD-ROM		CD-I	
	mode 1	mode 2	form 1	form 2
Synchronization	12 B	12 B	12 B	12 B
Header	4 B	4 B	4 B	4 B
Subheader	-	-	8 B	8 B
User Data	2048 B	2336 B	2048 B	2324 B
EDC/ECC	288 B	-	280 B	-

See form 1, form 2, mode 1, mode 2.

seek   The action of changing the location of a pointer and then finding the specified location.

seek latency Delay between a request for search action and arrival at the location sought.

service request   A request made of the kernel by an application to perform a specific activity.

simulation   A mock-up of how a CD-I application will play, using whatever hardware and software may be necessary.

single-medium system In computers, a system architecture based on the use of a single medium which carries all the software needed for a given application. In CD-I for example, all the program data (video, sound, text and computer), application and driver software is held on the CD-I disc itself. Only the basic operating system kernel is stored - in ROM in the base case CD-I player - external to the disc.

sleep A process execution state where the process will be inactive until a specific amount of time has passed or an interrupt is received.

sound attribute In CD-I, a particular property assigned to all or part of the sound information e.g. language, bandwidth.

sound group In CD-I, part of the user data field in an ADPCM audio sector. Contains four sound units, each consisting of four identical sound parameter bytes of 8-bits and 28 data bytes. Each ADPCM audio sector has 18 sound groups.

sound macro A predefined sound or sound sequence stored in computer form.

sounding Memory area that preloads audio data from disc.

soundmap A memory area allocated by UCM for storage of ADPCM audio data.

sound parameters Filter and range values describing the characteristics of a sound group.

sound quality level Four levels of audio quality are defined. These are CD-Digital Audio with a bandwidth of 20 kHz and 16-bit sampling, CD-I Level A, 17 kHz bandwidth with 8-bit sampling, Level B, 17 kHz bandwidth with 4-bit sampling and Level C, 8.5 kHz bandwidth with 4-bit sampling.

sound unit A unit consisting of sound parameters and sound data bytes.

spatial correlation A characteristic of visual images that there is a high degree of similarity between two adjacent images in a sequence of given images.

speech quality In CD-I, the fourth level of audio quality. A bandwidth of 8.5 kHz is obtained using 4-bit ADPCM at a sampling frequency of 18.9 kHz. Comparable with AM broadcast sound quality. See audio quality level.

sprites Small images on a screen, movable under program control, and normally ranging from character sets or cursor shapes to specific patterns as in computer games.

stamper A recording mould used to press gramophone records or optical discs.

storage capacity The amount of data a particular store can accommodate, generally specified in bytes. Storage can also be quantified in terms of the type of information stored. The over 660 MByte storage capacity of a Compact Disc, for example, can hold the data needed to reproduce over 160,000 pages of typed text, 72 minutes of the finest quality sound, or some 5000 video-quality natural pictures.

medium	storage capacity capacity (bytes per unit)	access times
RAM	64k...8MB	<1 sec
floppy disk	128kb...4MB	30msec
hard disk	5MB...200MB	30msec
magnetic tape	25MB...1200MB	minutes
Compact Disc	650MB	<1 sec

straight PCM mode In ADPCM, the PCM mode used as predictor for signals having high frequency characteristics.

subcode channel In Compact Disc, one of eight sub-channels, referred to as P to W, which exist in parallel to the main channel. They are used for control and display information.

subheader In CD-I, a field indicating the nature of the data in a sector, thus allowing real-time interactive operation. See sector structure, synchronization. The field defines file number, channel number, submode and coding information. The subheader can be thought of as a series of real-time switches that reduce load on the microprocessor and co-processors and save decoding time.

submode byte The submode byte defines global attributes of the sector.

subscreen The horizontal portion of a single frame that can use different decoding and resolutions than other subscreens in the same plane.

superimpose Place a computer-generated image over an image from another source. See overlay.

switching overlay A technique in which every pixel in the displayed image is selected from one or other of the corresponding source images.

symbol In Compact Disc, the basic unit of digitized data, parity and subcode data. Initially 8 bits long, is expanded to 17 (143) bits by eight-to-fourteen modulation.

synchronization   The process of maintaining common timing and coordination between two or more operations, events or processes. In the CD-I system, featuring simultaneous pictorial, sound and text information, the synchronization of the various elements which form the total presentation is an essential task of the applications program, under the control of the CD-I operating system, CD-RTOS.

The data stream from the disc, which carries the information to be interpreted by the CD-I player for presentation on the video screen and reproduction by the hi fi system, consists of a series of sectors. A subheader at the beginning of each sector, directly following the data stream synchronisation and header fields indicates to the CD-I controlling microprocessor the nature of the information in the user data block which directly follows the subheader information. This user data information can be part of the application program (or the boot or start-up information for the application). It can be data for interpretation by the video processor as pictorial information, or by the audio processor as audio information. Or it can be text or other program data to be interpreted by the main microprocessor.

Based on the indication contained in the sub-header, the microprocessor switches the user data block to the appropriate circuit.

It is then the task of the application program to instruct the micro-processor how to handle the information once it has passed through the relevant decoding process. In some cases, such as for CD-DA music tracks, the output data will be switched directly to the audio output channels.

In the case of applications program or computing data, the information may well be stored in the main memory, while video data will pass to the video memory to build up a picture for later display.

The synchronization function of the application then relates the various outputs from these data buffers to data coming directly from the appropriate decoding circuitry, to ensure that they are all presented in correct synchronization.

In the example illustrated, the synchronization data control triggers the video memory to indicate when the picture transfer from the disc is complete, and then to pass the background picture of the clouds, house and earth to the screen. At the same time, the sound data representing rain is passed to audio channels. At the appropriate moment, the overlay of the lightning flash is triggered to the video output, and a short time later, the related sound of thunder is passed to the sound channels.

A second example shows a cooking program, with the additional complexity of multilanguage text in synchronization with multilanguage speech. The other elements which make up the presentation - background, clock, smoke and a moving head and body - are all synchronized in a similar manner to the first example.

synchronization field In CD-ROM and CD-I, the first 12 bytes of a sector containing synchronization information.

synchronization primitives   Low level mechanisms for use by application software to perform synchronization of the video, audio and data sectors with themselves.

synchronization signals In CD-I, real-time software interrupts, often generated by a device driver during hardware interrupt processing when a predefined condition has been met.

synthesis parameters The parameters used to regenerate audio information from data stored in a compressed or encoded format.

system modules   Program modules that are required for the CD-I system to function. These include the kernel, file managers and device drivers.

system state   A special state of the processor which allows execution of privileged instructions; synonymous with the "supervisor" state of the 68000 family of microprocessors. File Managers and device drivers always execute in system state.

system text In CD-ROM and CD-I, a message processed by the operating system without the need to load and process any special text processing application program.

table of contents Subcode information defining the sequential number, start, length and end times of tracks on a Compact Disc, together with their type, i.e. digital audio or data. The table of contents is contained in the Q sub-code channel of the lead-in area of all Compact Discs.

TOC See table of contents.

track (1)In recording and computing, a path along which data is recorded, on a continuous or rotational medium, e.g. magnetic tape, magnetic disc. In video recording the track is diagonal on the tape. In magnetic discs the data is recorded on a series of circular tracks. (2) In Compact Disc, a sequence of contiguous data, the beginning, length, mode and end of which are defined in the table of contents, which is held in the Q subcode channel of the lead-in area of the disc. The two types of tracks currently defined are the CD-DA track according to the CD-DA specification and the data track according to the CD-ROM specification, which is also used in CD-I. In CD-DA the length of a track is related to playing times between 4 seconds and 74 minutes.

tracking The following of a track by a readout or pick-up device.

transition (1) In filming and video, change from one image to another. (2) In digital technology, change of state in a bit stream.

transition area A short sequence of DYUV codes which have been pre-calculated to make the transition from the YUV values in the surrounding image just preceding a partial update to those at the left edge of the update proper. Each line of a partial update must similarly be terminated with a transition area.

transparency bit In CD-I, a dedicated bit controlling overlay transparency in the cursor plane and the RGB (5:5:5) plane.

transparency control The three transparency mechanisms used to control the display of superimposed image planes.

treatment An overview of a proposed CD-I title, including information on the logistics involved in the title's creation.

trigger, trigger-bit A bit in the submode byte of the subheader that is interpreted by an application to cause synchronization of various events.

U One of the two chrominance components of a video signal containing color information.

UCM See User Communications Manager

user application A program or related set of programs designed for the user of a system, rather than for programmers or service technicians. See applications software.

user communications manager The CD-RTOS file manager which provides the software interface to the user and output devices on a CD-I player.

user data In CD-ROM and CD-I, data supplied by an information provider for an application. As such, includes retrieval software, but not information the information provider may be required to supply to facilitate authoring.

user data field In CD-ROM and CD-I, a 2048-byte-long portion of the data field in an addressable sector, dedicated to user data.

user interface The interface through which the user and a system or computer communicate. Includes input and output devices such as a keyboard, a hand control, a touch pad, a touch screen, aprinter and a display, and also the software-controlled means by which the user is prompted to supply data needed by the application, and by which he is notified of his errors and how to correct them.

user number A code or password by means of which an authorised user can gain access to a computer or to stored information. For example, the PIN, or Personal Identification Number used for authorising bank transactions.

user shell In computers, a program between the operating system and application program on the one hand, and the user on the other, to enhance the manner of information presentation and command.

user state The state of the machine when user processes execute and user related requests can be processed.

V One of the two chrominance components of a video signal containing color information.

vertical retrace period Time during which the vertical field scan on a TV screen returns to the beginning of the next field.

video data In CD-I, data related to one or more units of video information as encoded in DYUV, RGB (5:5:5), CLUT or Run-Length encoding techniques.

video data sequence The basic unit of image data loaded by a command in the real-time control area (RTCA). It typically contains the pixel data for an image or a partial update to an image.

video error concealment In digital video, a technique to reduce the visual effect of disturbances arising from erroneous video data.

video input-output The facility for video input as well as output from a computer. With frame grabbing, for example, video signals can be input to the computer for additional processing, and then output to the display. See frame grabber.

video quality level The reproduction quality of a video signal. CD-I provides for four video quality levels viz. natural pictures, RGB (5:5:5) graphics, CLUT graphics and Run-Length-coded animation.

visual effects function In CD-I, one of the set of functions, such as signal mixing and color palette control, used to achieve visual effects.

voice grade audio information Audio information of a quality sufficient for reproducing the human voice, normally having a bandwidth of 4-8 kilohertz. See speech quality.

volume A disc that forms part of a set, or album.

volume identifier Field of the File Structure Volume Descriptor identifying the name of the CD-I disc (volume)

wipe The replacement of one image by another during a period of time by the motion of a boundary separating the visual parts of the two images.

world disc A CD-I disc on which the video data is encoded in such a way that it can be played and displayed on any CD-I player, irrespective of 525 or 625 line TV standard.

world execute (file attribute bit) This bit of the attribute field of a directory record if set to one specifies that any user can execute this file.

world read (file attribute bit) This bit of the attribute field of a directory record if set to one specifies that any user can access this file.

WORM See write-once, read-many(-times) medium.

write-once medium Medium on which data, once written, cannot be erased to permit re-writing e.g. card, paper tape and DOR optical disc.

write-once, read-many (times) medium Synonymous with write-once medium.

write/read medium See read/write medium.

X-Y device Input device for entering X and Y coordinates, mainly used for accurate cursor positioning.

Y component The luminance or brightness component of a video signal.

yellow book Informal name for the CD-ROM specification.

YUV In video, symbol denoting the luminance signal (Y) and the two chrominance signals (U and V). See YUV encoding.

YUV encoding A video encoding scheme taking advantage of the human eye's reduced sensitivity to color variations as opposed to intensity variations. In each picture line, the luminance (Y) information is encoded at full bandwidth, while on alternative lines the chrominance (U and V) signals are encoded at half bandwidth.

zoom In video and photography the facility to enlarge, (zoom-in) or diminish (zoom-out) the area of interest in an image.

APPENDIX C: INTRODUCTION TO CD-RTOS AND INVISION

CD-RTOS is the operating system component of the CD-I system. It stands between application programs and the details of the hardware. If there are several programs running at once, it insulates them from one another.

CD-I is new, but CD-RTOS is a new name for a familiar and thoroughly tested operating system, OS-9. It was written for the 6809 microprocessor in the late 70's, and ported to the 68000 in 1983. Both the 6809 and the 68000 versions of OS-9 are widely used in process control and personal computing applications. Versions of OS-9 are available for several popular personal computers including the Tandy Color Computer and the Atari ST. The name is new and CD-RTOS includes extensive new I/O support, but the the operating system has years of experience behind it.

Most of the large body of OS-9 software can be adapted to CD-RTOS. These programs should run under CD-RTOS with no more changes than might be required to adjust them to a new terminal type. From the operating system's point of view the sophisticated CD-I hardware is "only" a collection of new I/O devices.

The diverse history of CD-RTOS brings some unusual functions to the CD-I player. The CD-I base case system will contain an operating system with the latent ability to turn the system into a serious computer. It seems improbable to use a CD-I player as a multi-user computer, but all that is lacking is a writable mass storage device (e.g., a floppy disc drive), and plugs for a few terminals.

The CD-I system does not simply copy data from the disc to its output devices. Except when it is emulating a CD-audio player, a CD-I system expects the application to supply a program that will run under CD-RTOS.

The program controls and modifies the data flowing through the system. It is the last point at which a CD-I designer can have control of the data, and the only point where the actual sequence of events in an interactive application is known. Imagination and craftsmanship in programming will improve the responsiveness of the application.

BASIC CONCEPTS

Processes

Operating systems like MSDos and the Macintosh operating system don't support multitasking. They can be forced to run a print spooling program, but only by following special rules while writing the spooler program. CD-RTOS is designed to run a large number of programs at the same time. There are no special rules or restrictions on print spoolers, or compilers, or clock displays, or any other programs that you might want to run concurrently.

The CD-I hardware requires multitasking support. There are four separate streams of data coming off the disc, plus a keyboard and pointing device that may be used at any time. While the system takes input from these six sources it must be able to simultaneously deliver output to the video and audio processors. All eight I/O activities must take place on demand. The CD-RTOS operating system handles much of the problem of keeping eight I/O balls in the air. Servicing all the streams of input and output seldom uses all of the processor's power, and the processor time that is not used by CD-RTOS is available to application programs. These programs need not use more than one task (tasks are called processes under CD- RTOS), but multitasking is the best way to ensure that all available processor time is used.

A skillful programmer can use multitasking and the other asynchronous CD-RTOS services to make applications run more quickly. If a program needs to wait for keyboard input, the programmer should ask himself whether there is some way to make use of the processor time until the input arives. Under CD-RTOS waiting for input doesn't use any processor time and even a fast typist doesn't enter more than about ten characters a second. The CD-I machine can do a great deal of work in a tenth of a second.

Modules

Programs are made up of machine instructions - code - and data. Code is kept in objects called modules which can be stored on discs, in ROM (Read Only Memory), or in RAM (Random Access Memory). Every module has a name, and when the module is in ROM or RAM the operating system can use a module's name to locate it.

Programs consist of one or more modules. The modules making up a program may be shared among several programs. They can also be loaded into memory when needed and deleted when a program needs the memory for something else. Both of these tricks save memory.

Programs written for CD-I systems should be exceptionally flexible. If the program is written as a number of modules it can be flexible without wasting memory on all possible options. For instance, a program could choose a display support module depending on the user's preferences (language, type of display, type of pointing device, and whatever else). The programmer would have to write separate modules for each display mode the designer wanted to support, but all those options would need to be programmed for in any case. By loading a tailored module the programmer can save the memory which would have been consumed by all the other alternatives. The program will also run faster by saving the time it would have spent selecting the right alternative every time display services were used.

The CD-RTOS operating system is built of a number of modules. This gives it tremendous flexibility. Adding support for new hardware to the operating system is a matter of changing or adding a few modules. If a vendor wants to sell a hard disc drive for a system running CD-RTOS, they will need to include two or three modules with the drive. The customer can connect the drive, load the modules into memory and start using the drive. There is no need to change the operating system when the system hardware changes.

Most modules contain program code or constants. Data modules are an exception. They can be created dynamically (All other types of modules must be loaded from a disc.), and they are used to hold variable information. They are excellent tools for inter-process communication and medium term storage. Data modules stay in memory until they are unlinked or the machine is turned off.

Input/Output
As far as possible, CD-RTOS has a consistent interface to all I/O devices. A program needs to name a file or device to open it, but the open returns a path number which is all the program needs for subsequent operations on the file. A program can get the the details about an I/O path if it requires them, but in many cases there is no need to know even whether output is going to a screen, a printer, or a floppy disc drive. Sometimes this is only a small convenience to programmers, but it can be wonderfully useful.

Directories
CD-RTOS is able to arrange files on random access devices in hierarchical directories to any depth. This is conceptually a simple idea, though the standard manila folder analogy becomes brutally stretched by the unlimited size and depth of directories. A disc, or any other random

access device, has a root directory which is always created when the disc is formatted. The root directory and every other directory contains a list of files and directories. You can name a file by giving the path list that reaches it.

Typing long path lists for every file would quickly make directories an unattractive organizational tool. The main CD-RTOS file systems support two default directories, one for executable files, another for all other files. Any path name that does not start with a slash (indicating a device name), will be taken relative to a default directory. If the file is opened for execution (as the load command would do), the execution directory is used. If the file is not opened for execution, the default data directory is used.

THE PARTS OF CD-RTOS

The base of the operating system is the kernel. This module supports the services that a sophisticated operating system cannot do without. Input and output are not handled by the kernel. It routes I/O operations to operating system modules called file managers.

File managers typically deal with device-independant aspects of I/O. The key file managers in CD-RTOS are CDFM and UCM. CDFM manages files on compact discs, and UCM (User Communications Manager) manages the CD-I user interface.

Other file managers from OS-9 are available for use in an extended player. There's a file manager called RBF (Random Block File Manager) which manages files on mass storage devices like hard discs, floppy discs, and RAM discs. Another file manager called SCF (Sequential Character File Manager) handles devices like terminals, modems, and printers. Nfm (Network File Manager) can be used to build a network of CD-RTOS and OS-9 computers.

File managers can be independent of the details of the hardware they use because there are other operating system modules called device drivers that handle the details of the I/O hardware. RBF doesn't care whether it is handling a floppy disc, a hard disc, or a RAM disc. All those details are handled by device drivers.

Device descriptors tie a name to a device driver, a file manager, and some constants. Programs give the operating system the name, and the operating system hooks the parts together to give the user the right file manager, device driver, and the address for the I/O hardware.

PROGRAMMING FOR CD-I

The CD-I File Manager

A Review of the Hardware

To understand the CD file manager (CDFM) you need to understand some facts about discs and disc players. The low- level format of a CD-I disc and the mechanism that plays it are are exactly the same as for CD-audio. Because of this similarity CD-audio discs can be played on a CD-I player, and CD-DA tracks from a CD-I disc can be played on a CD-audio player.

The technology used for CD-audio was intended to offer about the same functions as a record player. Random access to tracks of a recording, or maybe a little finer, was sufficient. Delays of about a second when the player skipped tracks were acceptable. Since CD-audio was designed with these limits in mind, and CD-I was designed to be compatible with CD-audio, it's not surprising that it's difficult to make disc players with fast random access.

Some CD players seek faster than others, but the data rate of all CD players is fixed by the specification. This is one of the ways that a CD-I player is exactly the same as a CD-audio player. The player reads the disc just fast enough to feed CD-DA information to an audio processor. There is no way to increase the data rate on a CD-I player, and the only way to decrease it is to ignore some of the data.

Let me put the performance of a compact disc in computer terms. For simple reading, a compact disc player delivers data about five times as fast as a disc drive, but any substantial seek is about ten times slower than for a disc. A CD-I player can read the disc briskly but only for sequential access.

Playing Real Time Files

CD-I type-A audio must be delivered to the audio processor half as fast as it can be read from the disc. This gives some unused bandwidth for other data, but only if the data can be reached without a seek.

The best way to arrange data for fast access by any disc-like system is to group the data close together on the disc. A CD-I system makes it easy for the disc designer to group related data. A single file can contain computer data, sound, and video. The CD-I hardware and CD-RTOS can separate the different data streams and deliver them where they are needed.

Real-time data is information that must be processed quickly. CD-I allows disc sectors to be tagged as real-time data. Though any data may be marked with the real-time attribute, it is intended for time sensitive data like audio codes. Because the real-time attribute is attached directly to each real-time sector, files can contain ordinary data and real-time data mixed in any convenient way.

The real-time sections of a file are called real-time records. CDFM will treat real-time records as ordinary data if it is asked to read them, but if a CDFM play command is used instead, the real-time attribute will be honored.

The CDFM play commands are unlike any operations on a conventional file system. A play command opens the flood gates and lets data from the disc pour into memory as fast as the hardware picks it out. The program that issued the play command can direct the stream of data, but the only way it can effect the data rate is by changing the rules used to select data from the disc. The program must keep up with the data.

The program has little control of the flow of data, but the rate can be set when the disc is designed. If the designers only put a stream of monaural level-C sound into some part of a real-time record, the data rate will be only one sixteenth of full flow. The authoring system will arange the data on the disc so the system can pick out each sector at the right moment, and CDFM will see to it that they are delivered to the application or the audio processor almost instantly.

The disc designers could have tucked other data between those audio sectors. The play command divides the data flow from the disc into four streams. Three streams go to blocks of memory provided by the application. These streams are for audio, video and program data. The fourth stream goes directly to the audio processor. The data on the disc is tagged so CDFM will know where to direct it.

Each logical record in a real-time record has a channel number that was assigned to it when the disc was designed. The CD-I system supports 32 channels of which 16 can be used for any type of data. The other 16 channels may be used for anything but audio data. CDFM can be directed to select logical records from a file based on their channel numbers.

CD-I channel numbers are not like television channels. A program need not select a channel for a read or play command. It can choose to receive any bundle of channels, even all of them.

Careful assignment and subsequent selection of channels can give a single real-time record many different appearances. There are 4,294,967,295 different ways to choose channels - plus one if we count choosing no channels at all.

The set of channels (the channel selection mask) can be changed between real-time records. Since a real-time file can be made up of many real-time records, the number of ways a real-time file can be played is actually much greater than four billion.

Probably the simplest thing to do with a compact disc is to play strictly sequential audio data. This can be done almost without program involvement. The three streams of data that CDFM buffers for the program can be empty or ignored. The only active stream is from the disc to the audio processor. The program to play a disc with a couple of hours of music could be as simple as an open for the music file and a play command.

The three streams of real-time data that the play command directs to memory are stored in buffers that are described by a play control block (PCB) and three play control lists (PCLs). The play control block contains control information for the play command and pointers to the three play control lists.

The play control lists contain the detailed information that CDFM uses to manager buffers. Each entry in a play control list contains control and status fields, a pointer to a buffer, a pointer to the next play control list entry, and a signal number that CDFM will send to the program if it encounters a trigger interrupt on the disc or when it fills the buffer.

A program may fail to process a buffer in the interval between the time CDFM fills a buffer and the time the next sector is ready. When a buffer is full CDFM will move to the next play control list entry. If there isn't a buffer ready for the data, CDFM will send the data directly to the output processor for that type of data (this really only makes sense for audio data). It can't wait for the program to empty a buffer. To avoid this problem, a programmer should put two or more entries in each play control list. With at least two entries in the list, CDFM can be filling one buffer while the program is processing the contents of another buffer.

The arrangement of links in a play control list is entirely up to the programmer, but linking the entries into a loop should work well. The CDFM will work its way around the links filling buffers while the program follows behind.

When a play command is issued the file manager starts an asynchronous activity. The activity is an operating system service on behalf of the program - not a process. A program can control the play command through the play control block, but the actual operation takes place inside CDFM.

The play in progress can by monitored through a control block that contains the current position in the file, but it's more in keeping with CD-RTOS style to give the play command some signal numbers so the file manager will be able to notify the calling program when buffers are filled, when a "trigger" in the disc file is encountered, and when the command terminates.

The most extreme use of the asynchronous nature of the play command is to start the CD-I file manager playing a file then ignore the progress of the command. This would be the best way to play a file of strictly audio information routed directly to the audio processor as was discussed earlier. While data travels from the CD to the audio processor the microprocessor is free to do anything that doesn't directly involve the audio processor or the disc. While the file plays, the microprocessor might run a graphics display or even a text editor.

CD-DA Files

CD-DA is simple 16-bit digital audio. It is the highest fidelity audio encoding method available to CD-I designers, but it uses the entire bandwidth from the disc. Since no other data can be mixed with CD-DA data, the disc is inaccessible while CD-DA is being played. This limits the microprocessor and the video processors to whatever data is in RAM before the play command starts.

A special CDFM command plays CD-DA files. The command always routes data directly from the CD to the audio output. The only connection that the CD-DA play command makes between a running CD-DA play and the calling program is a signal that can be sent by CDFM when the play is done.

There are a few brute force ways to influence a CD-DA play in progress. The play can be paused or the disc can be ejected. The position in the file can be determined to within a second by using a getstat system call. This is enough to implement the functions that most CD-audio players offer, but no more.

Reading CD-I Files

In many ways CDFM makes CD-I files seem like RBF disc files. They have a directory hierarchy, and files can be opened and read in random order. Since CDFM ignores the contents of a file when it is processing a read request, read is a good way to get simple data off the disc. Reading is particularly appropriate for files that contain only computer data, but files containing audio and video information can be treated like conventional files when that is called for.

The User Communication Manager

The User Communication Manager, UCM, is the CD-RTOS file manager that handles the four devices that are used primarily for interaction with the user: video, audio, keyboard, and pointing device. The connection to the keyboard and pointing device is fairly ordinary. The connection to the audio output is moderately unusual, and the interface to the video output can be complex and wonderful.

Keyboard Input

A read request to a UCM path will return characters typed at the keyboard. A program can either issue a read and wait for input or ask UCM to send it a signal when keyboard input arrives.

Since CD-RTOS will buffer keyboard input whenever it is entered, a read request might be satisfied immediately with data in the keyboard input buffer. A program can ask UCM how much data is waiting in the buffer and use that information to decide whether to simply read from the keyboard or ask to be signaled when more data arrives.

The Pointing Device

The simplest way to use a pointer device is to use the PT- Coord function to get the current coordinates of the pointer. If an application needs to track the pointing device, it must poll UCM for the current location frequently enough to respond smoothly to any movement.

Polling steadily for the pointer location is wasteful. Getting the coordinates twenty times per second might be enough to track the pointer responsively, but it would be useless except when the pointer is in motion. CD-RTOS lets a program track the pointer without wasting time polling when the pointer is at rest.

The program can ask UCM to send it a signal every time the pointer location changes. A program that uses this facility need only ask for the pointer coordinates only when they change. This prevents the program from wasting time checking the pointer when it is not moving. It also adapts the rate at which the program checks the coordinates to the speed of the pointer. The program will check the pointer exactly often enough to track it accurately.

Audio Output

Audio output revolves around soundmaps. A soundmap is a data structure that UCM uses to store data that can be routed to an audio processor. The information in a soundmap is encoded in sound groups, just as it is stored on a disc. Internally, a soundmap is a block of sound groups, the number of sound groups in the block, and a code that indicates the way the sound is encoded.

A UCM function creates soundmap data structures. It returns a pointer to a soundmap which can be used to load the structure with audio data. It also returns a soundmap identifier which is the name by which UCM recognizes the soundmap.

All UCM sound-manipulation operations are performed on soundmaps. UCM will also output soundmaps (and only soundmaps) to the audio processor of your choice.

Two UCM instructions merge a pair of soundmaps into a third soundmap. Two monaural soundmaps can be combined into a stereo soundmap, or two stereo soundmaps can be mapped into another stereo soundmap. These operations don't perform any actual mixing of the sounds represented by the soundmaps (in the sense of an audio mixer). They only copy channels intact from soundmap to soundmap.

Ordinarily the length of time a soundmap will take to pass through the audio processor is determined by the audio coding method and the number of sound groups in the soundmap. A programmer can lengthen this duration vastly by installing loops in the soundmap.

A UCM function can put a loop in a soundmap by giving the number of the first and last sound group in the loop and the number of times the loop should be submitted to the audio processor. A loopback could be used to extend a uniform sound for a specified interval, or to repeat a bounded sound a specified number of times. The sound of a basketball being dribbled could be made by looping around the sound of one bounce.

The features of the audio loopback are not yet precisely defined. It might be possible to use several loops in one soundmap. Perhaps a roar of applause followed by rythmic clapping and finally a dying patter of individual claps could be compressed into an applause loop, an intermediate section where the rythm begins, a rythm loop, and a dying out section with many little loops. More complex rythmic effects might be made with sequenced and nested loops.

There are two UCM functions that can be directed at audioprocessors without mentioning soundmaps. One function amounts to a volume, pan, and balance control. It controls the attenuation of each path in the audio processor: left to left, right to right, left to right, and right to left. An audio processor can also be turned off - thereby interrupting any soundmap that is active.

The main source of soundmap data is the CDFM play function, though programs are free to generate soundmap data. Generating or manipulating soundmap information is difficult. It would be an ambitious project to generate or modify ADPCM codes in software, and soundgroups must be stored as ADPCM data.

There is a special case of ADPCM data that is comparatively easy to work with. If the filter coefficients in type-A ADPCM soundgroups are set to zero, the result can be manipulated like 8-bit PCM data.

Video Output

Drawmaps are the UCM data structure for video output. They can be loaded by a CDFM play command or under program control. A wide selection of operations on draw maps is supported by UCM. These operations can combine drawmaps in many ways, draw characters or graphics, and display the drawmaps with great flexibility.

Text

UCM supports multiple text fonts and supplies several tools for writing text into a drawmap. These tools are divided into two groups: one treats a drawmap like a video terminal, the other uses a drawmap as the bit mapped object that it is.

Any program that works with a video terminal can be converted to use UCM's terminal emulation mode. The emulation supports all the features of a simple terminal including line editing and character attributes. The screen is controlled by writing text and control codes to it with the CD-RTOS I$Write command. UCM terminal emulation is not the best way to use the full power of CD-I video, but it is a familiar interface with enough power for many applications.

UCM also provides tools that draw text on the screen. These commands take a precise location and a text string. The text string is drawn on the screen with the baseline of the first character at the specified location. One of the text drawing commands will justify the string to a given length. Control codes are not used with the text drawing commands. This leaves more work for the program, but it lets characters be placed at the exact locations the program specifies. The terminal emulator only allows positioning to a line and column.

Fonts

Extensive support for text fonts is built into UCM. Fonts are described by data modules that must be in memory when the fonts they describe are in use. The system can have up to 4 fonts active at any time with a total size of up to 64K characters.

A character is always designated with a single code, not a font number and a character number, nevertheless each character code selects a font as well as a character. The way a character code selects a font and a character within the font depends on the active fonts and the way UCM interprets the code.

UCM has three modes modes for interpreting character codes. Eight-bit codes range from 0 to 255 - enough for most character-based languages - maybe enough for a few type styles. Seven/fifteen-bit codes represent 128 characters in eight bits. The high-order bit is reserved as a mode switch. If the high-order bit is on, 16 bits are used for the code. The seven/fifteen-bit method generates character numbers zero through 127 with eight bits per character, and 32768 through 65535 with 16 bits per character. This gives enough codes for oriental languages and many type styles. Careful assignments of character codes will let frequently used characters be represented with the 7-bit codes. Sixteen-bit codes don't offer the compression opportunity of seven/fifteen-bit coding, but sixteen-bit coding is simple and it can represent 65536 characters.

If one font can contain as many as 65536 characters, why does UCM bother to support four fonts at a time? The reason for multiple fonts is tied up with the way fonts are coded. Each character in a font has a number, a bit map, and a width. All the characters in a font share height characteristics, a proportional/monospace attribute, and a coding method. To get variety in some attributes (like character height) an application must use several fonts.

Since UCM does not use a separate font code for each character, each font/character pair must have its own number. This requires some care when numbers are assigned to characters in a font (which is done when the font module is made). UCM will not tolerate overlapping codes between fonts.

Operations on Drawmaps

The User Communication Manager has a variety of tools for copying a section of one drawmap into another drawmap. The simple tools copy or exchange rectangular regions between two drawmaps. Other tools offer variations on the simple ones.

There are special copy and exchange operations that accept a transparent color. These operations will not copy pixels that represent the transparent color. The pixels that would have been replaced by the transparent color are unchanged by these operations. This gives UCM the ability to simulate some of the transparency operations supported by the video hardware.

Rectangular areas or individual pixels can be copied in and out of a drawmap. The UCM converts the image data into a standard array of pixel information when it reads it out of a drawmap, and converts it from pixel form to the drawmap's internal form when it writes data into the drawmap.

An irregular write operation permits updates of selected parts of a drawmap. The operation updates each line in a given range, with the extent of the update specified on a line-by-line basis. The update for each line has a location and a length. Lines that don't need updating can have a zero-length update.

The operations on drawmaps can be used to conserve disc bandwidth. When a portion of an image must be updated, that portion can be read (or played) from the disc and used in an drawmap-update operation. In some cases partial updates can give the appearance of full-screen full-motion video.

The Graphics Cursor

The video processors support a graphics cursor, a 16x16 image plane that sits in front of the other planes. The UCM offers a high-level interface to the graphics cursor hardware. It includes functions to control the existence, location, shape, color, and blinking of the cursor.

The conventional use of a graphics cursor is as an on-screen analog to the pointing device. As usual, CD-RTOS does not enforce this convention. Any use for a mobile 16-bit-square image plane is valid for the graphics cursor. Perhaps it would be an easy way to represent icons when they are in motion?

Clipping Regions

Part of a drawmap can be given a name. The part is selected and the name assigned by creating a region. If two or more regions are defined in a drawmap they can be combined with a region intersection, union, difference, or exclusive-or operation. A region can also be moved within a drawmap. Regions can used as clipping regions or they can be drawn on the drawmap.

When a clipping region is "set" in a drawmap no drawing operation will be allowed to change the drawmap outside the clipping region. This is a useful feature for window support and graphics operations. Notice that clipping really clips. Things that are clipped off are not stored anywhere. If the clipping region is changed, the image will not be updated. (If you need clipped data retained use a mask.)

Drawing Commands

The User Communication Manager offers a good set of graphics functions. The scope of the graphics support is typical of a good graphics package.

A Partial List of Drawing Commands

Set Drawing Pattern
Set Pattern Alignment
Set Color Register
Set Clipping Region
Set Pen Size
Set Pen Style
Draw a Dot
Draw a Line

Draw a Polyline
Draw a Circular Arc
Draw an Elliptical Arc
Draw a Rectangle
Draw an Elliptical-Corner Rectangle
Draw a Polygon
Draw a Circle
Draw a Circular Wedge
Draw an Elipse
Draw an Eliptical Wedge
Draw a Region
Bounded Fill
Flood Fill
Copy Drawmap to Drawmap

Displaying Drawmaps

UCM does not have a function that simply displays the contents of a drawmap on the screen. The program must provide a display control program (a program that will be executed by the video processor). In its simplest form the display control program directs the video processor to display a range of lines from a drawmap. When its full power is used, a display control program (DCP), can operate the video processor as a special effects device.

One part of a display control program is executed every time the video processor starts to display the screen (50 or 60 times per second); this is called the FCT (Field Control Table). Another part of the display control program is executed for each scan line; this is called the LCT (Line Control Table). The same codes are used for the FCT and LCT. They differ only in when they are executed.

Instructions placed in the FCT will be executed once each time the display is refreshed. The FCT must include an instruction that points the display processor to the LCT of the line that should be displayed at the top of the screen. If there are any display other attributes that can be set for the entire screen, the FCT might be a good place to set them. For instance, the selection of the top image plane might be done here.

There must be a DCP for each of the two image planes (or paths). Each path controls the parameters that effects it, but path 0 has a few extra instruction codes that control both planes; e.g., plane order.

UCM supplies a series of commands that manage the components of a DCP. These commands give programs a uniform interface to the DCP, but the application program is responsible for composing and modifying the DCP programs.

The DCP instructions that link LCT to FCT, and LCT to LCT are the only instructions specifically supported by UCM. These instructions are useful for scrolling and split screen effects.

Most special effects are performed by manipulating DCP programs. A cut from one image to another can be done by changing the top plane in the FCT. A wipe can be done by changing the top plane one line at a time or by using a matte. A fade can be done by decreasing the image contribution factor of both planes over time. A dissolve involves increasing the contribution of one plane while decreasing the other.

Display Parameters Controlled by the DCP

Image Coding Method
Transparency Control
Plane Order
Backdrop Color
Transparent Color (for each plane)
Mask Color (for each plane)
Image contribution factor (for each plane)
Mosaic Control (for each plane)
Color Lookup Table (for each plane)
Matting (for each plane)

DCP instructions can control video parameters on a line by line basis, but they can't directly affect anything other than the video processors. For instance, there is no DCP instruction to read the disc or modify a drawmap. There is, however, a DCP instruction that causes a signal to be sent to the responsible program. These signals can be used to synchronize program activity with DCP activity. UCM exposes the power of the video processors to application programs by making display control programs the responsibility of programs. This does not mean that every program that displays video data must include explicit code that manages the DCP. InVision provides a layer over most of UCM, hiding many of the details of screen management.

The Real Time Record Interpreter
Real-time records can contain a RTCA (Real Time Control Area). These control areas contain computer data that describe the operations that should be used to process the data that follows. The language used in the

RTCA is not as powerful as direct use of the UCM, but it is a convenient way for each record to encode directions for its own processing.

A trap handler named RTRI (Real Time Record Interpreter) interprets the codes stored in the RTCA. An application that wishes to use the RTRI must open a real-time file and call the RTRI to play a specified number of real-time records. The RTRI will handle the details of playing the file asynchronously.

RTRI Functions

Soundmap Functions
Create Soundmap
Output Soundmap
Stop Audio Processor
Conceal Soundmap Error
Close Soundmap
Mix Mono to Stereo
Mix Stereo to Stereo
Set Soundmap Loopback
Set Attenuation

Drawmap Functions

Create Drawmap
Set Drawing Origin
Copy Drawmap to Drawmap
Exchange Between Drawmaps
Copy with Transparency
Exchange with Transparency
Irregular Write
Read Drawmap
Write Pixel
Read Pixel
Conceal Drawmap Error
Close Drawmap

Graphics Cursor Functions

Position Graphics Cursor
Show Graphics Cursor
Hide Graphics Cursor
Graphics Cursor Pattern
Graphics Cursor Color
Graphics Cursor Blink

Clipping Region Functions

Create Region
Region Intersection
Region Union
Region Difference
Region Exclusive Or
Move Region
Delete Region

Drawing Functions

Set Drawing Pattern
Set Pattern Alignment
Set Color Register
Set Clipping Region
Set Pen Size
Set Pen Style
Set Transparent Color
Draw a Dot
Draw a Line
Draw a Polyline
Draw a Circular Arc
Draw an Elliptical Arc
Draw a Rectangle
Draw a Rounded Rectangle
Draw a Polygon
Draw a Circle
Draw a Circular Wedge
Draw an Ellipse
Draw an Elliptical Wedge
Draw a Region
Bounded Fill
Flood Fill
Draw from Drawmap

Fonts and Drawing Text

Draw Text
Character Code Mapping
Get Font
Activate Font
Deactivate Font
Release Font
Draw Justified Text

Display Control Program Functions

Create FCT
Read FCT
Write FCT
Read FCT Instruction
Write FCT Instruction
Delete FCT
Create LCT
Read LCT
Write LCT Read LCT Column
Write LCT Column
Read LCT Instruction
Write LCT Instruction
Delete LCT
Link LCT to FCT
Link LCT to LCT
Execute DCP

Drawing Information Functions

Set Interlace Mode
Calculate Text Length
Relative Char. Positions
Return Font Data
Return Glyph Data
Justified Char. Positions
Is Pointer in Region
Get Region Location

Terminal Emulator Functions

Write
WriteLn
Set Output Drawmap
Set Mapping Mode
Activate Font
Deactivate Font

Pointing Device Functions

Get Pointer Coords.
Signal on Pointer Change
Release Device

Keyboard Functions

Read Line
Read
Signal on Data Ready
Release Device
Check For Data Ready

Functions for Reading the Disc

Load Soundmap
Load Drawmap
Read Data
Play to Audio Processor
Seek to Block

Housekeeping Functions

Read RTCA
Set Alarm
Set Channel Mask
Exit
Delete Label
Open Path

RTRI instructions include an opcode, control information, and parameters. The opcode specifies one of the functions in the RTRI function table or an application-specific function. These instructions are executed by the RTRI in response to signals.

Instruction Map

Op code	S. Signal	T. Signal	R. Count	Sig Stop	Parm Length	Parms

Op Code   Selects a RTRI function

S. Signal   Signal to send on completion of function

T. Signal   Signal to trigger this function

R. Count   Kill this instruction after it has executed R count times.

Sig Stop   Stop activating instructions for the trigger signal after this instruction.

Parm Length Length of the instruction's parameter area

Parms   The parameters for this RTRI instruction

Every RTRI parameter has a length and a label. The length is for the parameter's initializing value. If the length is zero the function has no initializer. If the label is zero, the value of the parameter is not available except to the function executed by this instruction. If the label is non-zero, the parameter is shared among all the instructions refering to that label number.

The flow of control in an RTRI program is not like an ordinary program. There is no sequence of instructions that will be executed. All the instructions listen for their trigger signal. When the signal appears they queue up to execute.

Signals come from all the usual CD-RTOS sources and from the RTRI itself. Each instruction can send a signal when it completes.

Picture each instruction as an active entity. They listen for their signal and move to the execution queue whenever they hear it. When an instruction is through executing it might send a signal to call on other instructions to execute.

The instruction-termination signals can be used to make a sequence of RTRI instructions execute. The first instruction can send a termination signal that triggers the second instruction, the second instruction can trigger the third, and so forth. Meanwhile any signals from outside RTRI can trigger their own instruction sequences.

If an application needs a function that is not provided by the RTRI, the function must be added to the RTRI instruction set for that application. The application program should include code that implements the new function. The function can be bound to an RTRI opcode by calling the RTRI trap handler with the new opcode and the address of the corresponding routine.

There is a speed penalty incurred by the RTRI (as with any interpreter). When performance is the highest priority, ordinary programs can do better than the RTRI.

The strong point of the RTRI is small programs. Its policy of loading the instructions to handle each real-time record with that real-time record is especially efficient.

Since RTRI instructions hide asynchrony to some extent, it may prove easier to write correct programs for the RTRI than to write them in the C language.

Non-Volatile RAM File Manager

A small amount of non-volatile RAM is included in the CD-I base case hardware. CD-RTOS includes a special file system designed to have modest storage overhead for the non-volitile RAM.

The non-volatile RAM file manager (NRF) is a simplified version of RBF. The most noticable missing feature is directory support. There is a single NRF directory which maintains a list of NRF files and their attributes. Other NRF directories cannot be created.

CD-RTOS imposes no restrictions on the use of NRF files, but programmers should respect the limited non-volatile storage on a base case system.

USER INTERFACE FOR DEVELOPMENT SYSTEM

Applications on a consumer CD-I system may offer the user an interface designed specifically for the application or they may use the InVision user interface. InVision is a set of enhancements to UCM and a user interface library that implements a loose standard for user interactions.

Designers are free to use InVision or modify it to give their applications a special flavor. Provided that the flavor is not too special, designers and users will be able to enjoy some variety and the benefits of a standard interface.

THE PROGRAMMER'S VIEW

I have been discussing programming in abstract terms. Unfortunately there are some important issues that CD-RTOS programmers must understand. This section will touch lightly on some important details.

Processes

CD-RTOS starts processes with a fork command or a chain command. These differ in that chain replaced the current process with the new process while fork creates a new process and leaves the parent process running.

The parent process can specify the number of I/O paths that the child will inherit, the contents of the child's parameter area, an amount of extra memory for the child's stack area, and the priority the child should run at. The fork command returns the process number of the child.

When a process starts, almost all of the MPU registers are set to significant values. Most important are the stack pointer, the PC, and a static storage pointer. Many operating systems don't give new processes a static storage pointer. Since CD-RTOS is a multitasking operating system which does not require memory management, programs must be able to run anywhere in memory. The operating system tells them where it placed there static storage, and the programs take it from there.

Processes can have considerable influence on the way they are scheduled. They can instruct the operating system to ignore them for a length of time with a sleep command, they can wait for a child process to terminate with a wait command, and they can change their scheduling priority with a SPrior command.

Memory

One symptom of multitasking (without memory management) is that a region of memory can be cornered by memory allocated to other processes. When that happens to a program's stack area, the amount of the stack memory can't be increased until the other process releases the memory that is blocking the stack. CD-RTOS has a system call to change the size of the stack allocation (like a Unix sbrk), but this call will fail if memory contiguous with the stack allocation is not available. Another system call that allocates blocks of memory wherever it can find them should be used whenever possible.

Synchronization

The CD-RTOS file managers make extensive use of signals to communicate with programs. Signals are the software equivalent of interrupts. When a signal is sent to a process, the normal execution of the process is interrupted and control is transferred to the process's signal handler.

A process can give CD-RTOS the address of a function which the operating system will call each time a signal is directed at the process. The signal function will be entered with the signal number as a parameter, and the A6 address register set to a value that was specified when the signal function was identified. By convention this register is the base address for static storage, but an assembly language programmer could use it for something else.

A process can mask signals that it doesn't wish to receive. This is done automatically when a process is in the signal function. Signals that are not received are queued for later attention. A process that doesn't wish to handle signals can elect to mask signals, or to catch and ignore them. If it does neither, any non-zero signal will kill the process.

Subject to some security restrictions, processes can send signals to one another. Inter-process signals work exactly like signals from file managers.

Where Signals Come From

UCM	keyboard interrupt
UCM	keyboard kill
UCM	keyboard data ready
UCM	mouse motion
UCM	FCT signal
UCM	LCT entry signal
UCM	Done with soundmap
CDFM	End of play
CDFM	Play buffer full
CDFM	Play hit a trigger
Other programs	application-specific
CD-RTOS kernel	Alarm signals

CD-RTOS supports another synchronization method called events. Events have names and values and are accessible to any process that knows their name. A process can wait for an event to reach a certain value, or a value within a range. CD-RTOS commands set or increment the value of an event. It is simple to use events as semaphores, and with some imagination they can address almost any synchronization problem.

The primary job of a program in a CD-I system will usually be routing real-time data. Since this is a signal-driven activity, programs are likely to be bundles of functions and processes written for speed. Writing this type of program is not like ordinary programming. Debugging signal-driven programs is just nasty.

Modules

Programs for CD-RTOS must be position independent. The operating system supports multitasking, and gives modules no way to specify where in memory they should be placed. A program must assume that it could be located anywhere in memory and that its variables could be located anywhere else. Position independant code can be written for

68000-compatible processors, and compilers for CD-RTOS will generate correct code so far as they are able, but programmers should keep inthe back of their minds that code and data can be at different locations each time a program runs.

Whenever possible CD-RTOS programs should be re-entrant. Once a module is in memory it is convenient for the operating system to let every program that needs the module use the same copy. This is possible provided that the code and constants in the module are not modified by any process that uses it.

The Role of Programming

Most CD-I systems will probably look more like stereo systems than computers. But they are computers - powerful computers. A CD-I application can include a tremendous amount of data, but the data will be presented to the user by a program. It is probably best if users forget that their CD-I appliance is a computer, but a CD-I designer must not.

No household appliance (except, perhaps a telephone) has had anything close to the computing power of a CD-I system. We can only guess how the tool will be used.

INVISION

INTRODUCTION

InVision is an example of an object-oriented multi-media user interface designed for Compact Disc-Interactive (CD-I) players. Other interfaces will be available in due course. Since InVision is intended for a consumer product, it is designed to be simple and easy to use by the user of a CD-I player. For the content provider, not only does InVision provide access to standard UCM functions, it adds several powerful new capabilities to the CD-I environment.

ARCHITECTURE

The diagram shows the base case CD-RTOS software modules and the InVision modules and their relationships to each other. The thick lined boxes represent InVision modules while thin lined boxes represent CD-RTOS modules.

InVision consists of three modules, a Display Manager, a Presentation Support Library, and a Visual Shell. The Display Manager is a CD-RTOS subroutine module for the UCM file manager and provides access to the video, audio, pointer and keyboards drivers like the User Communications Manager. It also manages screens to allow more than one application to run at a time and action regions for simplifying input.

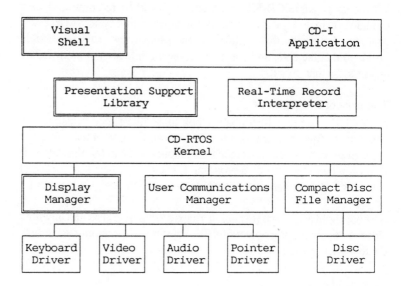

The Presentation Support Library is a CD-RTOS trap library. This collection of subroutines further simplifies the task of manipulating the display and obtaining input from the user. The Presentation Support Library provides requesters, which are standardized ways of asking questions of the user and controls, which are standard ways of getting switch and volume control input from the user. The Presentation Support Library includes a set of visual effects functions, a set of internationalization functions to assist applications in being country independent, and functions to maintain and determine certain preferences of the user.

The top level of InVision is the Visual Shell. The Visual Shell is the only part of InVision that the user will actually see. It essentially forms the control panel of the CD-I player. The Visual Shell is fully customizable by the player manufacturer. In addition to its main function of starting the play of a disc, the Visual Shell can execute a set of small utilities called accessories. Accessories perform functions such as setting preferences, setting a clock, or controlling other parts of an audio-video system. The accessories that are included with a CD-I player may also be determined by the manufacturer.

THE DISPLAY MANAGER

The InVision Display Manager (DSM) is a CD-RTOS subroutine module to the UCM file manager and provides InVision's interface between the CD-RTOS kernel and the CD-I video, audio, keyboard and pointer drivers. It is also the application's basic interface to those drivers. In addition to providing access to standard UCM functions, the Display Manager introduces two new capabilities to the CD-I environment, screens and action regions.

SCREEN MANAGEMENT

The Display Manager provides screens so that more than one application can be in progress and providing information to the user of the CD-I player. Since there is only one physical display for the system, multi-tasking causes several applications to both attempt updates on the same display. The Display Manager gives each of the applications a 'logical screen' on which to display their output. At any given time only the top screen is visible on the display and the application running on that screen is the only interactive application available.

The screen management functions are based on the display control program functions supported by the video driver. In addition to providing access to the video hardware's field control tables (FCT's) and line control tables (LCT's) in much the same way that UCM does, there are functions which coordinate the use of those elements in relation to the logical screen.

Each screen appears as a single display control program to the application that is using it. It is a collection of at least two LCT's, one for each plane. All of the functions for creating, deleting , reading, writing and linking LCT's provided by UCM are also provided by the Display Manager. This part of the design of the Display Manager has been kept the same as UCM so that applications have virtually the same ability to generate visual effects, including the ability to pre-master the data for those effects.

Functions are also provided to associate a FCT's with each screen. These provide the ability to load instructions which affect the entire screen or load a large number of color look-up table registers in the hardware. When a screen is to be the one displayed its FCT's are executed as the current hardware display control program.

There are functions for showing, hiding, raising and lowering screens. These functions are used to switch between screens when running multiple applications. For example, a user could be interacting with one application and want to access the Visual Shell for a moment. The Shell screen will become the visible screen allowing interaction with the Visual Shell. When the user us done they can return to the original screen and interact with the application again.

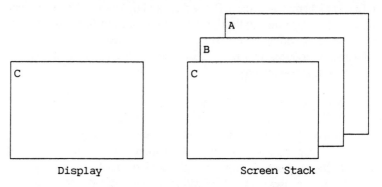

Display   Screen Stack

A diagram of a collection of screens is shown along with a diagram of how the screens would appear on the display. The screens are maintained in a stack mush like a stack of paper. In the figure, the individual screens are the same size and are aligned with each other and the display. Since screen C is at the front of the stack, it is the only one that is visible on the display.

The next diagram shows how the screen stack and display change when a new screen is created and displayed. Whenever a screen is created it is added to the top (front) of the stack.

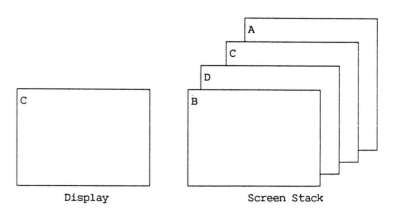

Display   Screen Stack

The last diagram shows how the screen stack and display change when a screen (screen B) is raised. Screen B moves to the front of the stack and becomes visible.

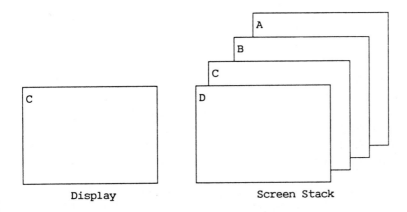

Display   Screen Stack

MESSAGE MANAGEMENT

The Display Manager provides a simple method of inter-process communication. This facility is mainly used by the Display Manager to transmit packets of information about pointer activity to applications. It is general enough, however, that it may be used by applications using InVision to send messages to each other.

The Display Manager provides each process using InVision with a queue for these messages. Several functions are provided for manipulating the message queue. The send function adds a new message to a queue. The receive function retrieves a message from the queue. Specific types of messages may be selected with the receive function. There is also a function to determine if a message or a particular type of message is in the queue. Particular types of messages may also be flushed from the queue.

ACTION REGIONS

Action regions provide a mechanism for condensing and organizing the continuous stream of coordinate and trigger data that comes from the pointing device. By using action regions, applications can define areas of the screen where the application is notified of the specific area where the pointer activity occurred and the type of pointer activity that occurred.

Action regions are based on the region mechanism provided by the video driver. Whenever a screen is created a conceptual third plane, called the action region plane, is created and placed in front of the two image planes provided by the CD-I video hardware. This action region plane can also be thought of as the cursor plane, since cursor movement is generally associated with pointer movement.

The Display Manager continuously monitors the stream of data coming from the pointing device, determines which screen and action region the pointer activity is associated with, and sends a message to the application associated with the screen and action region. The message contains the action region identifier, coordinate, and type of pointer activity. Pointer entering action region, pointer exiting action region, pointer moved, trigger up and trigger down are the possible types of pointer activity.

The Display Manager provides a very powerful set of functions for manipulating action regions. The most basic of these is the move function. Any action region may be moved to any position in the action region plane. This allows the possibility that action regions might overlap each other. To resolve these conflicts, the Display Manager maintains the action regions in a stack. An action region higher in the stack has priority over one lower in the stack. The create function adds new action regions to the top of the stack and the delete function removes action regions from the stack. The raise function moves an action region to the top of the stack while the lower function moves one to the bottom. The activate function causes the Display Manager to consider the action region when it searches for an action region to be associated with a pointer activity. The de-activate functions causes the Display Manager to ignore the action region in its search.

Action regions are also hierarchically organized. Child action regions may be created and associated with their parent. Whenever child action regions are moved, they are positioned with respect to their parent. These child action regions are maintained in stacks which are attached to the parent, yielding a tree of action regions. When the Display Manager searches the tree for an action region associated with a pointer activity, it performs a top-down recursive search, looking for the highest priority action window lowest in the tree which contains the coordinate of the pointer activity. The action region functions manipulate the child stacks exactly like parent stacks.

The hierarchical organization of action regions allows the creation of groups of action regions which can be treated as one unit. Whenever a function is performed on an action region, the same action is performed on its children. If an action region is moved, all of its children move with it. Raising, lowering, activating or de-activating an action region causes the same thing to happen to all of its children.

THE PRESENTATION SUPPORT LIBRARY

The Presentation Support Library is a collection of high-level functions for simplifying application development for CD-I systems. Many of the concepts found in traditional computer based user interface libraries are included in the Presentation Support Library but are tailored to make use of the multi-media capabilities of the CD-I system and oriented towards a consumer based product. The main functional capabilities of the Presentation Support Library are:

- Controls. Controls allow an application to obtain input from the user using objects similar to switches and volume controls.

- Requesters. Requesters allow an application to ask the user a question and obtain a reply.

- Visual Effects. Functions are provided to simplify the task of generating visual effects such as mattes, wupes, fades, dissolves and cuts.

- Internationalization. Functions are provided for an application to separate country dependent data such as prompts from the application so that it may be country independent.

- Preferences. Functions are provided for maintaining user preferences such as language or nationality.

CONTROLS

Controls are a high-level mechanism for obtaining input data from a user of a CD-I player. They provide applications with a mechanism to draw objects on drawmaps and associate action regions with them. These objects may also change appearance depending on the type of pointer activity in the action region. When the sequence of pointer activity in the action region required by the control occurs, an application defined function can be executed to take action based on the value of the control. The concept of controls in the Presentation Support Library is very general to allow the application great flexibility in generating this type of user interaction. An application may create its own control behavior or use the standard control behaviors.

The most common types of controls are buttons and variable controls. The Presentation Support Library provides three types of standard control behavior, pushbuttons, switches and variable controls. The application is able to customize these controls by providing the image data for each of the states of the control. This makes it possible to have controls built from natural images. The figure shows an example of a screen for a CD-Audio player accessory. This accessory uses pushbuttons for the play, pause, stop, fast-forward, rewind and eject keys. Variable controls are used for the volume, balance, bass and treble controls.

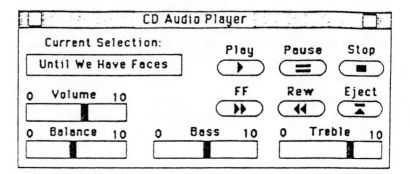

Pushbutton type controls behave in a manner similar to a momentary contact switch in that they are used to initiate a specific action by the application. Pushbutton controls appear to the user in one of four states depending on pointer activity in the control's action region and the application. The disabled state is set by the application and is used to tell the user that the button will not do anything. When the button is not disabled and the pointer is not in the control's action region it is in the normal state. When the pointer enters the control's action region the control enters the highlighted state, signifying to the user that the pointer is on the button. If the user then depresses a trigger button, the control goes to its active state. When the user releases the trigger button, the control is returned to normal state and an application specified function is executed.

Switch controls behave similar to an on-off switch. Switches controls have a value associated with them, specifically, on or off. Switches controls appear to the user in one of five states. disabled, normal on, normal off, highlighted on and highlighted off. As with pushbuttons, switches can be disabled by the application. When the switch is not disabled and the pointer is not within the control's action region, the control is either the normal off or normal on state. When the pointer enters the control's action region it enters one of the highlighted states. When the user depresses and releases a trigger button, the value of the control is changed from off to on or from on to off. Whenever the value of a switch is changed an application specified function is executed. The new value is passed as a parameter.

The variable control is used to implement dials and slides and may have one of many values associated with it. Visually, the image of a variable control has two parts, a background and a moveable part. The moveable part appears to the user in one of three states, disabled, normal and highlighted. As with pushbuttons and switches, the application may disable a variable control to signify to the user that the control will not do anything. When the control is not disabled and the pointer is not in the control's region, the control is in the highlighted state. If the user depresses a trigger button, the user can move the moveable part of the control by dragging. The application can specify two functions to be executed by this type of control. One is executed while the button remains down and the pointer is moved. The other is executed when the trigger button is released. Both are passed the value of the control as a parameter.

REQUESTS

Requests, like controls, are a high-level mechanism for obtaining input from the user of a CD-I player. Applications use requests to present a question to the user of the CD-I player and get a response to a range of choices. Requests are typically used at decision points in an application where the user can guide its flow. They are similar to the pop-up of pull-down menus supplied with computer based user interface toolkits. While the application has complete control of the appearance of requests, including the ability to supply actual image data, the question and choice behavior of it is not changeable. The figure shows the CD-Audio player accessory with a request on it, asking the user to select a song to play.

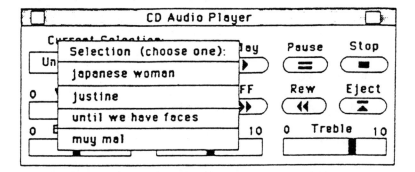

Requests consist of a question and several possible responses. When the request is drawn on a drawmap, an action region is associated with each choice. Each choice can appear to the user in one of three states, disabled, normal and highlighted. When the application disables a choice it signals the user that the choice is not a valid one. If a choice is not disabled and the pointer is not in its action region, the choice is in the highlighted state. If a trigger button is depressed and released then an application specified function is executed. It is passed the choice as a parameter.

VISUAL EFFECTS

The Presentation Support Library includes a number of functions to simplify the generation of such visual effects as wipe, fade, dissolve, matte and cut. The Field Control Tables and Line Control Tables which control the display contain parameter information in the form of instructions. Some of the visual effects functions generate lists of instructions which are suitable for writing into LCT's. One of these functions takes a drawmap and some coordinate information and returns a list of "load video start address" instructions which, when written to and LCT, will cause the selected portion of the drawmap to be displayed. Another takes a region created by the video driver and returns a list of "load matte register" instructions for writing into anLCT.

The other visual effects functions perform timed writes to LCT's. For doing fades and dissolves, there is a function which automatically generates a "set image contribution factor" instructions and writes them into the LCT at a rate specified by the application. Other functions write lists of instructions specified by the application on a timed basis.

INTERNATIONALIZATION

Since the CD-I market is international in scope, a significant number of applications will need to be country independent. The largest area of need for this is when applications prompt users for input using requesters or controls and in the display of textual information. To help solve this problem the Presentation Support Library provides resource modules. Content providers can store country dependent information in these modules. All an application need do is obtain the resource module for the correct language and use the data in it. A small number of functions are provided for properly formatting date, time and money strings according to individual countries' standards.

PREFERENCES

The Presentation Support Library maintains a file on the CD-I player's non-volatile RAM. It is mused to store the user's preferences. Preferences are simply parameters which affect the operation of the CD-I system which can be adjusted by the user. One of these parameters is the nationality of the user. This should be consulted by the country independent applications so they can determine how to present information to the user in a way that he is culturally accustomed to. Other parameters are key delay time and key repeat time.

THE VISUAL SHELL

The most visible part of InVision is the Visual Shell. The Visual Shell is the first program that the user interacts with when he turns on the CD-I player. The Visual Shell is designed to be the control panel of a CD-I player. Its main purpose is to start the play of discs and start the various accessories.

The Visual Shell is created using a request. The choices given in the request correspond to the accessories that are available on the player. The Visual Shell is fully customizable. When it is executed, the Visual Shell accesses a resource module that the manufacturer has included in the ROM. This module contains the image data for the background screen, the data required by the request and the names of the individual accessories that may be executed. The Visual Shell then waits until the user either inserts a disc or selects one of the choices on the display using the pointing device.

Small programs, called accessories are also provided with the Visual Shell. The programs are used to set devices such as a clock or maintain data in the preference file, or use the CD-I player as a CD-Digital Audio player. What accessories are provided with a player is determined by the player manufacturer. If a remote control bus is available on a CD-I player it could become the centerpiece of an audio-video system. Accessories could be provided that control each component on the bus.

Further information on InVision can be obtained from Microware Systems Corporation, Des Moines, Iowa, USA.

INDEX